KU-549-904

Criminal Women

Autobiographical Accounts

Diana Christina, Jenny Hicks, Josie O'Dwyer, Chris Tchaikovsky and Pat Carlen.

Edited by Pat Carlen.

Polity Press

This collection © Diana Christina, Jenny Hicks, Josie O'Dwyer, Chris Tchaikovsky and Pat Carlen, 1985.

Chapter 1 © Chris Tchaikovsky, chapter 2 © Diana Christina and Pat Carlen, chapter 3 © Jenny Hicks and Pat Carlen, chapter 4 © Josie O'Dwyer and Pat Carlen, 1985.

First published 1985 by
Polity Press, Cambridge, in association with Basil Blackwell, Oxford.
Reprinted 1986, 1988, 1991

Editorial Office: Polity Press, 65 Bridge Street, Cambridge, CB2 1UR, UK.

Basil Blackwell Ltd, 108, Cowley Road, Oxford OX4 1JF, UK.

Basil Blackwell Inc., 432 Park Avenue South, Suite 1503, New York, NY 10016, USA.

All rights reserved. Except for the quotation of short passages for the purposes of criticism and review, no part of this publication may be reproduced, stored in a retrieval system, or transmitted, in any form or by any means, electronic, mechanical, photocopying, recording or otherwise, without the prior permission of the publisher.

Except in the United States of America this book is sold subject to the condition that it shall not by way of trade or otherwise be lent, hired out or otherwise circulated without the publisher's prior consent in any form of binding or cover other than that in which it is published and without a similar condition including this condition being imposed on the subsequent purchaser.

British Library Cataloguing in Publication Data

A CIP catalogue for this book is available from the British Library.

ISBN 0-7456-0087-5
ISBN 0-7456-0088-3 Pbk

Library of Congress Cataloging in Publication Data

A CIP catalogue for this book is available from the Library of Congress.

Typeset by Pioneer, East Sussex
Printed in Great Britain by Antony Rowe Ltd, Chippenham, Wiltshire

Contents

Acknowledgements

Jenny Hicks would like to thank her two mothers for their continuing support and love. She would also like to thank all the charitable trusts which have supported Clean Break; and the Women's Committees of the Greater London Council (GLC) and Camden Council. The financial support of these bodies has enabled several ex-prisoners to get employment.

Josie O'Dwyer would like to thank Paul, Lynn, Colin and Liz, (wardens at the Kathryn Price Hughes Hostel); Dee, (Probation Officer); and all the members of Women In Prison. Finally, she would also like to thank herself — for giving herself a chance, at last.

Chris Tchaikovsky would like to thank Sarah Cawthra of the Prison Reform Trust; Fiona McLean, General Services Advisor, GLC Women's Committee; Valerie Wise, Chair, GLC Women's Committee; and Jenny and Ben Clements for staying the course.

Pat Carlen would like to thank Doreen Thompson at the University of Keele for transcribing the tapes on which chapters 2, 3 and 4 are based and also for typing those chapters; Laurie Taylor for reading and commenting on two chapters; Orna Fiegel, Patti Lampard, Peter Carlen and Jill Carlen for performing a variety of services connected with the book's production; and editors Michael Hay, Helen Pilgrim and Michelle Stanworth for their enthusiasm.

Introduction

Pat Carlen

Criminal Women: Myths, Metaphors and Misogyny

Criminal Women tells the stories of four women who, in attempting to become women of their own making, became embroiled with the criminal justice and penal systems to such an extent that today, as non-criminals and non-prisoners, they are still subject to the misogynous mythology which inseminates stereotypes of female lawbreakers and women prisoners.

Explanations of female crime have usually been given in terms of the failure of individual women to adapt themselves to their supposedly-natural biological and/or socio-sexual destinies.[1] The implication has repeatedly been that it is the individual women who should change — rather than the social formations which impose restrictive and exploitative roles upon all women. As a result, in both criminological and lay explanations, criminal women have always been presented as being 'Other': other than real women, other than real criminals and other than real prisoners.

To the present-day reader the early theories of female criminality appear at their most benign to be faintly comical; at their most malignant to be blatantly sexist. For, despite the claims to scientificity of the nineteenth-century positivist revolution in criminology, the old Adam and Eve theory of crime persisted as far as women were concerned. From the end of the nineteenth century onwards the mysterious powers attributed to the witches of earlier centuries have been attributed also to the 'scientifically' diagnosed female criminal. Consequently, for the last hundred years or so explanations of female crime have oscillated between, on the one hand, positivist assumptions which tie women forever to their biology and, on the other, biblically-inspired superstitions which represent 'Woman' as the source of all evil. Lombroso and

1

Ferrero's book *The Female Offender* published in 1895[2] contained most of the stereotypical elements responsible for subsequent characterizations of women lawbreakers.

Lombroso and Ferrero assumed that all criminals are throwbacks to an earlier stage of human development and set out to investigate whether women criminals have physical stigmata that differentiate them from non-criminal women. As they had already conducted investigations that had led them to claim that male criminals bear marked signs of degeneration to an earlier evolutionary type, when they turned their attention to female offenders they used the same methods — studying pictures of women criminals and measuring and generally examining the physical attributes of women prisoners. As it turned out, they found too few physical stigmata to support their theory of the atavistic (under-developed) criminal. None the less, they still managed to theorize their findings from an evolutionary perspective. Women criminals, they argued, show fewer signs of degeneration than male criminals because women in general are less developed than men. In other words, women criminals have less far to fall. When a woman *does* commit crime however, she is, according to Lombroso and Ferrero, much more cunning about it and, ultimately, more evil (as the judge's characterization of Jenny Hicks in chapter three of this book suggests). Additionally, the woman criminal offends not only against society but also against her true nature . . . as rooted in her biology.

To be fair to them, Lombroso and Ferrero did implicitly distinguish between the psychological, anthropological and biological constituents of female subjects. At the same time, and because they persisted in conflating the two distinct notions of sex and gender, they never actually managed to break free from the belief that a woman's true and natural socio-sexual destiny is dictated by her biological attributes. Furthermore, as the retarded development of women in general was seen to stem from an inherent passivity and conservatism engendered by the relative immobility of the female ovule as compared with the activity of the male sperm, *then* the active woman criminal — the born woman criminal — must, according to the theory, be in essence non-woman, masculine.

But can women successfully compete in what is, according to

the male pundits a truly 'masculine' activity? Lombroso and Ferrero, like many other writers since, were reluctant to think so. Their theory was given a further devious twist. Noting that most known women criminals are petty offenders, they claimed that the majority of women are not capable of true criminality. Instead, women are occasional criminals who are first led into crime by stronger-willed male partners and are then grossly incompetent in the performance of the felony and easily apprehended and brought to court.

In the nutshell of Lombroso and Ferrero's theory of 1895, therefore, are all the elements of a penology for women which persists, right up to the present time, in constituting women criminals as being both within and without femininity, criminality, adulthood and sanity. These misogynous themes not only occur again and again in the theories of women's crime but, what is more important, they continue to have a tenacious hold upon the minds of judges, magistrates and the administrators of the women's prisons. Before I make further mention of the ways in which judicial misogyny has repeatedly manifested itself in the courts I will briefly outline how Lombroso and Ferrero's assumptions have inseminated most subsequent explanations of female crime.

In 1907 the sociologist W. I. Thomas published his *Sex and Society* wherein he reinforced the Lombrosian biologistic position by again attributing essentially different personality traits to men and women.[3] Whereas men were seen to be more criminal because of their biologically-determined active natures, women were seen to be passive and less criminally capable. By 1923, when he published *The Unadjusted Girl,* Thomas had supplemented the biological approach with a social factors perspective.[4] He argued that as women have a greater capacity to love than men they suffer more when they do not receive social approval and affection. The 'unadjusted girls' are those who use their sexuality in a socially unacceptable way to get what they want from life. For Thomas then, the female criminal is the cunning sexual enchantress, she who foregoes the conventional rewards of domesticity by refusing to accept prevailing modes of sexuality. Obviously such a theory ignores not only the economic and cultural factors in prostitution but also the class system which has consistently ensured that certain working-class women have always been able to earn more by prostitution than they have by engaging in more conventional forms of labour and/or marriage. Thomas's solution, that delinquent girls should be made to adjust to their conventional female roles has, however, continued to be central to the philosophy of women's penal regimes both in the United Kingdom and elsewhere. That today's judiciary also endorse this solution was brought home to me in 1982 when I was repeatedly told by Scottish sheriffs and magistrates that a woman living with her husband and children would be much less likely to get into criminal trouble than would a woman leading a less conventional life.[5] Recent research into sentencing patterns has, moreover, suggested that sentencers translate these beliefs concerning the relationships between non-fulfilment of gender role-expectations and female lawbreaking into a sentencing logic which discriminates against women who are not, at the time of their court appearances, able to demonstrate that they are committed to conventional female roles.[6]

Otto Pollak, in his *Criminality of Women*[7] (1950) continues the theme of the cunning woman criminal and weaves it into his thesis that female criminality is masked. Why is female criminality masked? Because women are essentially more deceitful than men, are the instigators rather than the perpetrators of crime and — on top of all that — receive greater chivalry from the police and courts. Whence comes women's greater capacity for deceit? From the 'passive' role which, according to Pollak, they have to assume during sexual intercourse . . . and so on. Now, despite the absurdity of that last claim, Pollak's other claim — that it is police chivalry that accounts for the low rate of female crime — has had lasting effects. Again and again I have heard judges and magistrates argue that, as women offenders are given so many chances, those women who *do* end up in the dock or (worse) in prison must be very bad indeed.[8] The available empirical evidence as to the relationships between the actual incidence of women's lawbreaking and the rate of their official criminalization is extremely difficult to interpret but in a most recent review of it Stephen Box came to the following conclusions:

If the data provided in the *Criminal Statistics for England and Wales 1979* are standardised by controlling for the relative size of the male and female population between 15 and 64 years . . . then the following observations seem warranted.

The only offence where the female rate of conviction approximates that of men is shoplifting . . . A long way behind comes fraud and forgery — out of every five persons convicted, only one is female. . . . The official statistics, controlled for population size, show that the female rate of conviction is much lower than that for men — approximately only eighteen females are convicted for every hundred males convicted . . . Recent interpretations of self-report and victimisation studies on such 'conventional' crimes as murder, assault, arson, robbery, theft and burglary support the view that sex-differentials in conviction rates *reflect* albeit distortedly real differences in male and female criminal behaviour.[9]

When Box examined the evidence in relation to less serious offences however, he qualified the general conclusion, particularly with reference to young women and stated that:

It appears that with non-serious offences the official data under-reports the involvement of women, particularly young females who are more like their male peers than the official statistics reveal.[10]

None the less, the final judgement goes against both Pollak and the prevailing conventional wisdom of the courts. Box concludes his review of the empirical studies by commenting:

[Although] it would be wise to avoid dogmatic assertions . . . the weight of relevant evidence on women committing serious offences does not give clear support to the view that they receive differential, and more favourable, treatment from members of the public, police or judges.[11]

Conversely, and as has been argued by several authors,[12] when *young* women are seen to commit *relatively minor* crimes:

Juvenile courts are often transformed into stern parental surrogates who lock up their naughty daughters for behaving in ways which gain scarcely concealed approval when committed by sons.[13] [Cf. the story of Diana Christina in chapter two.]

In so far as Pollak directed attention to the social response to female crime in order to explain women's official crime rates he did indeed make a slight move away from biologism, but a link between biology and female criminality was maintained through much of the 1960s. As late as 1968 for instance, Cowie, Cowie and Slater[14] were arguing that, though delinquency in boys may be primarily caused by social factors, delinquency in young women is mainly a matter of biology, the most likely cause being a chromosome imbalance which makes delinquent young women act like men. So, although radical and non-positivist criminologies (for men) were already developing in the 1960s, it was not until the 1970s that the old explanations for women's lawbreaking began to be displaced. Even though Frances Heidensohn did remark in 1968 that 'a much more meaningful approach would take female deviance as an aspect of the female sex-role *and its relationship with social structure* [my emphases]"[15] it was not until Smart and Smart published their *Women, Sexuality and Social Control* in 1978 that there was a more sustained attempt to analyse women's lawbreaking and criminalization in relation to 'the complex and concealed forms of oppression and social control to which women are subject.'[16]

Yet attempts to establish a 'feminist' criminology have not been very successful and, it would seem to me, for two major reasons: first, because many feminist writers appear to have found it difficult to break free of the notion that crime is essentially a 'masculine' activity; second, because the searches for either a global theory of crime (female *or* male) or a special theory of female crime (global or not) are both theoretically unsound and politically ill-judged.

In 1975 two American criminologists each published a book discussing the relationships between apparent increases in women's lawbreaking and an assumed and generalized 'women's liberation'.[17] Surprisingly, although each author rejected the blatant biological positivism inherent in most previous explanations of women's lawbreaking, throughout both books there lurks a most unfortunate assumption: that as women acquire the same legal rights as men they will cast off their chains . . . and commit crimes like men. The assumptions of some feminist criminologists converge with the traditional and persistent assumptions of most judges and magistrates towards a consensualized view that liberation from male-related domesticity inevitably leads to an increase in women's lawbreaking (which is permanently under an erasure as being *really* a *masculine* activity). This view stems from the failure to distinguish analytically between: (1) lawbreaking and criminalization; (2) sex and gender; and (3) global theories of criminality and crime and historically-specific theories of lawbreaking and criminalization.

Just as it has nowadays become a truism for theoretical criminologists to assert that a distinction has to be made between lawbreaking and criminalization so, too, has it become a truism for feminist theorists to assert that a distinction has to be made between sex and gender. When criminologists talk about explaining 'crime' they recognize that, even at its crudest, criminological explanation has to pose at least two separate questions: why do certain people commit particular crimes and why are only certain groups of suspected lawbreakers regularly caught, sentenced and in some cases (not necessarily the most socially injurious) imprisoned? Likewise, when feminist theorists talk about 'women' they also know that, even at its crudest, feminist theory has to pose at least two separate questions: how do the conventional and binary 'sex' categories 'male' and 'female' differentiate between people on the basis of physical attributes? and how do the conventional and binary 'gender' categories 'masculine' and 'feminine' relate certain types of expected behaviour differentially to the always essentially putative 'males' and 'females'? However these conceptual distinctions tend to become conflated whenever it is assumed either that a *special* theory of 'women's crimes' is required or that a *global* theory of 'women's crime' is possible. For instance, as soon as it is assumed that a *special* theory of women's law-breaking is required then criminal activities have to be distributed to males and females on the basis of an activity's supposed 'masculine' or 'feminine' characteristics. (In fact what has happened has been much more crude: in circular fashion the crimes most frequently committed by women have been categorized as 'female' crimes, whilst the rest have remained 'male'.) When, on the other hand, it is supposed that a *global* (or universal) theory of either women's criminality or women's criminalization is possible then, also, it has to be presumed that social constructions of both sex and gender are unvarying between and within societies. Alternatively, if criminologists eschew explicit theoretical work and, instead, engage in studies which take either women's own self-definitions on their judges' stereotypes of them as being unproblematic, then again criminological explanation may find it difficult to break out of the gender trap. For, the still dominant (and often ambivalently romanticized) conception of 'crime' as an activity which is primarily the prerogative of males with an excess of *masculinity* influences both the self-definition of women lawbreakers and the assessments judges make of them. It is easy to see why certain young women may see their own lawbreaking as being a desirable encroachment upon one of the male routes to increased freedom, while their judges (for slightly different reasons), see women's lawbreaking as being both a manifestation of a *lack of femininity* and a justification for increased surveillance and severer punishment. In this way, both the explanations of the women themselves *and* the assumptions of the judges may lend credence to the thesis that an increase in women's liberation leads to more women committing more crimes. That is not a thesis to which I adhere when interpreting the autobiographical materials presented in this book. As Carol Smart argued in 1976, insofar as the crude 'liberation leads to crime' thesis does itself reinforce the conceptual straightjacket of the masculine/feminine dichotomy, such a thesis is, ironically, in itself, damaging to feminism.

> If some women *seem* [my emphasis] to be emulating men it is not because of the philosophy of the women's movement it is primarily because there are at present only two socially acceptable identities available to individuals, the stereotypical and polarised masculine and feminine models. If one is rejected the only other 'acceptable' model available is that of the other sex, there are as yet no socially legitimate alternatives.[18]

So, in commenting on the implications of the autobiographies which follow I would in no way wish to imply either that they show that all women who commit crime are protesting against sexism or that as women become more conscious of their oppression they tend to break the law. As far as its contribution to criminology is concerned I would make only two claims for this book. First, that the autobiographical accounts demonstrate in fine detail how, under certain material and ideological conditions, either law-breaking and/or other forms of deviant protest may indeed comprise rational and coherent responses to women's awareness of the social disabilities imposed upon them by discriminatory and exploitative class and gender relations.[19] Second, that the complexity of the accounts should call into question *all* of the monocausal and global theories of crime. For, as a result of the persistent assumption that a *special* theory of women's criminality is called for, theorists have not only been caught up on the horns of the misleading 'masculine or feminine?' dilemma, they have also, for much longer than has been the case in relation to 'crime in general', persisted in the quest for global, a-historical, monocausal and essentialist explanations. As Mark Cousins has pointed out, *any* explanations of a taken-for-granted 'female criminality' — whether those explanations be styled feminist, radical, marxist or whatever — *must*, by the nature of the project, be as reductionist and essentializing as the much-maligned biological ones.[20] So what *can* be said about women who are convicted and imprisoned for their lawbreaking?

In 1980 Mark Cousins argued that in order to theorize the relationships between the agency of criminal law and the organization of sexual difference, theorists should abandon stable referents for the categories 'male' and 'female' and 'masculine' and 'feminine' on the grounds that those categories are 'produced as definite forms of difference by the particular discourses and practices in which they appear.'[21] These particular discourses and practices have to be investigated and theorized if the social, legal and other ideological preconditions and effects of changing constructions of women's lawbreaking and women's imprisonment are to be both recognized and debated. The primary *assumption* behind such investigations would be that social constructions of sex and gender vary both across and within societies and that they have heterogeneous effects as they combine with other forms of differentiation, in particular as they combine with the differential effects of exploitative class and race relations. The primary *aim* of such investigations would be to unravel, and intervene in, the constellation of ideological and material circumstances which systematically condition the repeated lawbreaking and criminalization of certain women. At the same time, though, it would never be assumed that contemporary discourses and practices of gender differentiation *necessarily* play primary parts in the conditioning of that lawbreaking and criminalization. For instance, in some cases consciousness of economic marginalization (as a result of class position and/or racism and/or sexism) might be the main precondition for lawbreaking by women. Conversely, increased opportunity for some women to break the law might occur as a result of increased access to positions of occupational power and prestige. On the other side of the coin, it might be found that judicial misogyny can be directed at entirely different groups of women as changes in economic and ideological conditions provoke governments alternately and contradictorily to proclaim that women's place is in the home . . . or in the labour market . . . or in the home preserving the family (and thereby the society) from attack . . . or in the labour market helping the war effort . . . and so on. But, whichever way the judges jump, the point remains that there can be no one theory of women's crime because there can be no such thing as the 'typical' criminal woman — either in theory or in practice. This book is about four criminal *women* whose stories are important primarily because they deny the existence of the criminal *woman*.

The essential criminal woman does not exist. Women who break the law come from all kinds of backgrounds, though, as with male lawbreakers, those women who land up in prison are much more likely to have come from the lower socio-economic groups than from the higher ones.[22] Once their crimes become known, however, all women lawbreakers have to confront the myths which permeate both the criminal justice system and the prisons. The four autobiographical accounts presented in this book confront, question and, I think, ultimately deny the two dominant myths: that women criminals are either essentially masculine, maladjusted (to their 'natural' feminine roles) or mentally-ill; and that women's prisons are not real prisons at all but hybrids between mental hospitals and some rather saucy St. Trinians'.

The first three chapters confront the myth that female law-breakers, rather than being serious and intentional criminals, are nothing more than deviants from what are *supposed* to be their natural, biologically-determined socio-sexual roles and destinies. This myth is rooted first in a generalized misogyny which, rather than conceiving of little girls as being young female persons, conceives of them as being nothing more than embryo wives, mothers and sex-objects designed for the satisfaction of male desire. Second, and relatedly, it is at the root of the judicial misogyny which results in single women, divorced women and women with children in Care being more likely to receive custodial sentences than women who, at the time of their court appearances, are living at home with their husbands and children.[23] As a result of these sentencing patterns many women who go to prison do indeed suffer from homelessness, battering men and depressive illnesses; many also engage in addictive or compulsive behaviours. But these external characteristics of many *imprisoned* women do not necessarily mean that either they or their sisters in crime who do not receive custodial sentences are merely victims of either their biology or their circumstances. The stories of Chris, Christina and Jenny suggest the opposite; that crime can be consciously engaged-in by very intelligent women determined to be *successful* people. Certainly Chris (chapter one) Christina (chapter two) and Jenny (chapter three) rejected the conventional gender roles on offer to them, but this did not mean that they wanted to swap the conventional female roles for the conventional male ones. Rather, what they each wanted was the fun, independence and success which would lift them above the social disabilities imposed upon them as women. Although their individual quests for success took entirely different forms, each one of them, at some time in her career, deliberately engaged in lawbreaking as a way of either achieving satisfaction as a person or of resolving some of the problems or contradictions facing her as a woman. Chris, for instance, saw crime as a way of fulfilling her need for excitement and success; Christina, too, (although her story is *extremely* complex), on several occasions saw crime as being the best way of achieving her desire for kicks and high income; and, finally, Jenny, a working-class woman with an entrepreneurial flair, saw fraud as being the only method by which she could ever expect to succeed as a business woman in a man's world.

In chapter four, Josie O'Dwyer's account of how she survived Holloway and other women's prisons explodes the myth that women's prisons are caring places organized for the succour of the weak and the disciplined 'gentling' and reform of the maladjusted. Admittedly, Josie's experiences were extreme and, in so far as Chris, Christina and Jenny all approached their sentences very differently we can see that just as there is no typical woman criminal so, too, is there no typical female response to imprisonment. What *is* significant is that women's prisons, like men's, are *organized* to respond to difficult prisoners in all the ways that Josie so vividly describes. Josie's account also undoubtedly lends credence to T. C. N. Gibbens' 1971 claim that though many women in prison 'look as mad as mad can be, [they] are really reacting to prison life.'[24] However, the women whose prison careers are most likely to resemble Josie's are those very same young women who, like her, begin their custodial careers in their mid-teens. This is an extremely sobering thought at the present time when recent Prison Department statistics reveal that in the first six months of the operation of the new Youth Custody legislation (i.e. from May 1983 to November 1983) there was a 77 per cent increase in the number of females aged fifteen and sixteen received into youth custody centres as compared with receptions into borstal in the previous year; whilst 'for females aged seventeen to twenty there was a 17 per cent increase in receptions into youth custody centres in 1983 and an overall increase of receptions in prison department establishments.'[25] So, any readers shocked by the early penal incarceration of both Josie and Christina should not soothe themselves by thinking that it does not happen nowadays. Unless there is some radical change in the running of the women's prisons, today's teenage prisoners will continue to damage both themselves and others in their attempts to survive a custodial system completely unsuited to their needs.

Chris, Christina, Jenny and Josie have survived to tell their tales. Today, Chris, Jenny and Josie are workers for the campaigning group Women in Prison (WIP). Christina is a painter and poet. All of them have rejected lawbreaking. No longer do they see it as being either a satisfying mode of self-expression or a satisfactory way of making a living. But they still know why so many women do break the law and they know, also, just how difficult it is for isolated ex-prisoners to make their way back into an often uncaring society. It is because WIP does care that Chris, Jenny and Josie have struggled not only to chronicle their own stories but also to use those stories to inform their analyses of the almost insurmountable difficulties facing women who make the decision to turn their backs for good and all upon their criminal careers. So, although the following accounts chronicle some exciting and often very humorous times, some vicious incidents and some times of despair, they have, too, their moments of optimism, as, on the basis of their own experiences, the authors describe some of the more positive and creative ways and circumstances in which ex-prisoners can resolve some of the problems confronting them.

These stories of criminal women are vivid chronicles of the times in which they have lived. In presenting these chronicles we hope that they will not only destroy the mythology which inseminates contemporary stereotypes of criminal women; we hope, also, that they will contribute to the greater understanding of the complex and diverse responses which women can make when faced with the social disabilities imposed upon them by a class-riven and still deeply sexist society.

1
Looking for Trouble

Chris Tchaikovsky[1]

I do not intend to start by looking for social or psychological reasons why I turned to crime. This would lend weight to the view that criminality is either environmentally determined or born of mental disorder. For me it was neither. I did not really turn to crime, crime was all around me. It was only a matter of time before it turned to me.

Crime came in the shape of three ex-Borstal girls who had travelled to my home town to pick fruit. But although these hardened three were the supposed bad influence upon me this supposition was untrue. It was their misfortune to happen upon a teenager who, bored rigid in the provinces, was ripe and ready to lead them into breaking their hard-won Borstal-licensed freedom.

At the time I met my ex-Borstal allies I had hardly recovered from the shock of forcible schooling for six hours a day over a ten-year period. The frustration of losing all those previous happy days collecting snakes, feeding the beach ponies, swimming, running free! To me it was unbelievable that I was classroomed and expected to sit in small wooden stocks, not move (only it was not moving any more it was 'fidgeting') and be overseen by women more like Führers than Mothers. At school I was assailed with meaningless doodles that had wriggled their way from the sand to our blackboard and were called sums. At school I had to stand among friends in assembly who, like me, were not convinced that any of this was 'New Every Morning' as the hymn book told us. In assembly I became aware of, and did, unspeakably funny things and was not able to laugh, even quietly. I learned to laugh quietly soon enough, but my eyes always filled with tears and I shook — this ensured that I was spotted by the militia standing at the side. It was those first removals in shame from assembly to stand outside the head ogre's door that energized future rebellion, or more truly, future refusals to do what was required. Lines, bad reports, detention, no gold or silver stars and mean thumb-in-the-back teachers all combined to make sure that I was not going to take any of this schooling business.

With boys from the Grammar I hung a pair of Long Johns on the school flagpole (what was a school doing with a flagpole anyway?) . . . expelled Falmouth High. The next school was so awful that I refused to go altogether . . . expelled Bishop Blackall. At the next I buried a moth from the art room with full funeral honours — including a Mass and blacked-out teeth . . . expelled St. Thomas's. Other schools came and went. I did cycle to the gates at times, but I could not convince my legs that we should go in. Instead I cycled to the Pavilion on the sea front and talked to the pensioners. They were nice and talked about the war, the price of corned beef, the awful youth of the day and the five-bob funeral money that they saved with the Co-op every month. One elderly lady worried about the school truancy inspector on my behalf, but most of them thought it was fine that I hated school. They had hated it too and would go back over their schooldays, relishing all the terrible things that they had got up to. These happy sojourns were not to last. The schools' inspector did catch up with me and I was a reluctant visitor to a Child Guidance Clinic. What the purpose of this strange agency was is anybody's guess. Needless to say, I found little guidance and all that I can remember is being sent to a small farm, presumably to rest up and learn something.

On my first day, feeling good because I was sure — having checked out the place — that some adders were lurking there, I was taken by one of the Guiders to a shed wherein a bunch of sorry-looking hens were hanging upside-down. The Guider introduced me to another woman who looked suspiciously like a teacher, then proceeded to move along the flapping row stunning each hen with a hammer whilst the second woman moved behind her cutting off their heads. I was horrified and off back to my Father, who agreed with me that this was rather bizarre behaviour for a Guidance farm. He refused to send me back.

My Father often supported me in my refusal to accept various constraints that I thought were too much — he thought the same way. Also, as he had been told in my hearing that I had a reading age far in advance of my years he, like me, wondered what all the fuss was about. Of course I was not getting much of an education, but this was not important because a girl hardly needed brains when a man was sure to marry and keep her. In fact it could be a disadvantage, as most men did not like the brainy types. Ever the pragmatist, Dad gave me lots of work at home and through selling papers at the dock gates I picked up a little maths. I also read a lot and so was basically literate. If I read a lot I must be brainy and if I was brainy what was the point of attending school? I acquired what education I could along the way.

The last school I attended treated me differently from all the others. On my first day the Head called me in and told me that although this school was not keen to have such a reprobate, she would compromise a little to keep me there. I had come from a variety of High or Grammar schools; this school was for the not-so-bright. The top form were covering what I had happened upon in the second form on my occasional days of attendance. The Head suggested that I read stories to the first form. Maybe the school was short-staffed, or this was a clever Head, but, whatever the reason, I thought this was great. I prepared serious and snazzy stories for the first form and questions for them afterwards. And if any kid was brave enough I persuaded her or him to read a few lines. After school I treated the whole form — sweets for the good and Park Drive's for the mature. My lessons were popular. I attended other classes because I did not want to lose the 'teaching' and I happily completed the last year of my schooling.

A Different Kind of Trouble

29 May 1959 was one day after my fifteenth birthday. Childhood and school were over. I had four pounds in my pocket and I was on my way to the Cafe French in Old Compton Street, Soho. I forget how I knew this was the place to hit when you got to London, but The French lived up to my expectations. Foreign papers and people, Gauloise smoke and whispered conversations. It all smacked of Hemingway and Steinbeck and I felt truly at home. Not for long. I fell in with a black limbo dancer called Stretch. He was at least six foot six, friendly, and asked me if I had a place to live. I told him 'no' and he offered to put me up until I found one. I went home with Stretch complete with all the trust of a fifteen-year-old and in his case it was not misplaced. But Stretch had less

trustworthy mates and less than a week after coming to London for good I was on my way home to the family. A friend of Stretch had called by whilst he was out and had held a Black and White whisky advertising ornament over my head. Not content with frightening me out of my wits he raped me as well. I did have the good sense to lie quietly thinking that anything was better than those two china terriers cracking over my head, but the whole episode sent me home convinced that I would never see London again.

On my return home I decided that the only way not to work from dawn to dropping for my Father was to get a job. I joined the South Western Regional Hospital Board and I soon made friends with the other civil servants. The office supervisor and I attended church on Sundays and afterwards she would provide lovely home-made cakes. I also developed a crush on Mary Colston in the typing pool. Mary would walk by and be heard to mutter 'Hell's Bells and Buckets of Blood' at typing errors. I found this enchanting. I was still caught between a liking for the respectable and holy that I found in the office and for the vivid and villainous that I found in literature. The villainous won. After eleven months at the Hospital Board I thought my life was ebbing away and that if I did not leave I would turn without noticing into a filing cabinet. The final jolt came when Mr. Rose of 'accounts' retired on the Friday only to drop dead in his beloved garden on the Monday. I was convinced that his death was due to the shock that his heart must have received at not travelling to the office with him after all those years. This was not going to happen to me. Wages and pensions and five bobs to the Co-op? It all struck me as betting against life. I started saving for London.

Trouble Revisited

I met Trudy in the Duke of York where the Bohemians hung out. I had been going there for some time though I had not dared to speak to anyone. I had just listened, hoping that someone would eventually speak to me. I had taken a room in an hotel called 'Hotel' in Hammersmith, I had a job womanning a fruitpaste-smearing-upon-pie machine and I had pay to spend. I formed no friendships with my workmates because I thought that they were 'deadheads' who had never read Nietzsche and they thought I wore a fisherman's smock because I came from Cornwall.

Trudy was tall, thin, beautiful and definitely Bohemian. She spoke fast and with wonderful expressions like 'taking five' when she left for five minutes, 'splitting' when she left for longer and 'easing out' when she left altogether and went home. Trudy was a junkie. I did not know this for some time although she did appear agitated at times for reasons that I could not fathom. Soon I was 'running' for Trudy because she was either too strung out, too tired, or considered it too dangerous to go up West to score. Her 'man' was an abhorrent Chinese dealer who gave me the heroin openly in the middle of busy Gerrard Street, counting the money and cursing if it was a little short, but taking it anyway. I moved in with Trudy to a squalid flat in Brixton. I read *Confessions of an English Opium Eater* by De Quincey to try and understand her addiction, but I failed. For her part Trudy never fixed in front of me, supported her habit by hustling (but told me she had a rich sugar-daddy) and got more and more sick.

The junkies used to gather around an old lavatory in Tottenham Court Road. I waited there one night for Trudy, having scored her smack earlier. She was very late and I was worried. When she eventually arrived she looked terrible — blue-lipped, trembling and hardly able to stand. Trudy grabbed the small packet from my hand and rushed into the lavatory. She was so strung out that she did not notice me running down after her. I followed her into the cubicle and closed the door. I watched as she took out her 'works' — a dropper, syringe and a spoon. Trudy sucked some water from the bowl, mixed the powder in the spoon and lit a match under it. She was shaking so much that I thought she would drop the spoon so I held it for her whilst she searched for a vein. Trudy pressed and squeezed, like a cat frantically looking for fleas. At last she found one uncollapsed vein and fixed the junk. Everything serioused in my head. It was quite clear to me in that lavatory that Trudy was dying from heroin. At that moment, as if to compound the realization, the attendant started banging on the cubicle door, calling us filthy junkies and threatening to call the police. We left. Trudy was slowly coming around again to being the woman I knew, although I saw her differently now. Sick and sordid, a loser, a near-finished addict, she was 'other', different and certainly nothing to do with me. I packed the following day and left her a note which was, no doubt, cruel, self-righteous and|posturing. I knew no better. Yet again I had edged too close to the novels and it was all too much for me. I had walked into the nightmare world of Burroughs and I was not ready for it.

Real Trouble

Pubs lost their appeal almost as soon as I could legally enter them. In Exeter there was the added hazard that they attracted marines and soldiers who got drunk and belligerent, head-butted each other and generally spoiled any attempt at a good time. Teddy boys hung around on street corners while their middle-class counterparts bought cavalry twills and studied to be borough surveyors. I suspected them all of cowardice. The Teds moved on as soon as they saw the police. The budding surveyors moved on as soon as they saw the Teds. Only the Fair boys who came to the town did not seem to move on for anyone. But the girls who hung around the Fair boys read nothing but *Romeo* and *Valentine*, caked themselves in Panstick and, I heard, 'did it' behind the big wheel. They were not for me. Caught again between all the possible poors, I made, as usual, no close friends at all. I also nursed my London experiences and these ensured that I did not get involved with provincial small-timers, that I did not follow my sisters to the fair!

But Dirty Dot's was other. A small, dingy cafe had opened in the High Street. I had heard my Mother discuss its dreadfulness and I was there. Dot was a fifteen-stone, bearded, MA with an 'upper' accent who had, it was said, fallen on hard times because of a man. Dot, like her cafe, was indescribably filthy. She sat at the far end of it with a hugh chrome teapot in front of her and a rusted bucket beside. An assortment of fruit and Madeira cakes in cellophane were strewn around a Formica-topped plank which served as a counter. Loaves of bread, eggs and sausages were piled beside a double gas ring on which wobbled an enormous frying pan. In the centre, against a wall, was a dial-a-record juke box with a cracked glass dome. This juke box had the best records in town and Dot's was the least pretentious cafe in the place. The El Zamba was frequented by YCNDers and the juke had stuff like Edith Piaf singing *M'Lord*. The Milano was frequented by the Teds and smaltzed out perpetual Presley. Dot's had Del Shannon's

Runaround Sue, Duke of Earl, Take Good Care of My Baby, and
Eddie Cochrane's *C'mon Everybody.* Whilst all the other cafes
sold espresso coffee in glass cups, Dot did not think coffee would
catch on. I loved Dot's, but again I did not speak to anyone. I
played records, drank tea and listened to the conversations of the
seedy clientele — Trev Atkins, 'The Rat' and Limey Bull, 'The
Grass'. These two studied form and planned jobs which would
never come off, again and again spending money from 'the big one'
they would never do or see.

Dot liked me because, she said, I spoke well. She asked me if I
would like to work the door between ten-thirty and midnight. I was
quietly thrilled to be entrusted with the job and I took up my post,
looking as mean as I could in leather jacket and pale blue jeans.
Dot would raise herself up and oversee possible entrants through
the thick glass door and I would shake my head or open it
accordingly.

Dot deliberated for some time before sanctioning entrance to
Nicky, Chris and Pam because they looked just what they were,
three rough, tough, tattooed ex-Borstal girls. Chris was small with
peroxided clipped hair and was clearly the boss of the trio. Nicky
was thick-necked, crew-cut, fair, muscular and butch. Pam sported
an enormous beehive, teetered on five-inch heels and was very
pretty under ounces of dark brown make-up. The group were
visibly irritated about waiting to enter but, having registered Dot
and the situation, they did not complain. All three were dog-tired
and hungry after hitching from Essex to Exeter and walking, as
Pam said, 'half the bleedin way'.

The trio took a table next to my post, ordered fried-egg
sandwiches, put a good record on the juke box and began to argue.
Pam tidied her beehive and abused Nicky for not telling a lorry
driver that he was only getting a 'toss' for his two quid, some of
which was paying for the sandwiches. Nicky was just as adamant
that she had told the driver that there was to be no screwing and
that he, the steamer, was the liar, not her. Further, if Pam had
agreed to Nicky staying in the cab of the lorry the unthinkable
would not have happened. Pam was not convinced. Although she
agreed that she had not wanted Nicky to stay, this was, she said,
too strong; she couldn't perform with Nicky watching her and
what was Nicky anyway, some kind of pervert? Eventually Pam
cooled down but not before Chris confirmed that Nicky had told

the driver that it was no-go if he wanted the works and that she, Chris, had heard her set up the deal. If Pam had chosen to believe the steamer rather than believe Nicky it was Pam's fault not hers. Pam was appeased and informed the other two and the riveted clientele that it didn't matter really and that he was a right three W's anyway. 'Whip it in, whip it out and wipe it off,' she shouted and I laughed along with Dot and everyone else. Pam, like so many other hustlers I was going to meet, enjoyed conjuring the filthiest expressions, though at the same time this was combined with a purity peculiar to the man-loathing lesbian. Pam hated men, she found them gross, offensive and 'all the same'. Men wanted only one thing. Pam believed in romance not sex, and spent a good deal of her time writing, 'Pam loves Nicky . . . true' within hearts on walls. Chris and Nicky sent Pam up for her romantic leanings knowing that she enjoyed it and she, for her part, gave as good as she got.

I was fascinated by them. They did not fit in any group that I had ventured upon. They were outlaws. Rough, tough, loud, funny and, most importantly, completely different to the feminine women I had known. Even the men in Dot's treated them with respect. They, too, were villains, women maybe, but they knew what the inside of a cell looked like, they took their chances and hated the phoney world of the straights. For my part, I thought that they were heroines — free, wild, their own mistresses and scared of no-one. Their looks were outrageous, but not in any exhibitionist sense. Wherever they went, from the respectable they received nasty glances which they enjoyed; from the Teds shouts which they more colourfully reciprocated; and from the police overt interest which they both expected and ignored. They brought life to Dot's and an end to my provincial boredom.

Before long we were inseparable and planning a job. Chris, being the most intelligent of the three, was not keen and wanted them to finish their Borstal licence before burgling again. I was the prime mover although Nicky did not think that I had the bottle. Nicky also thought that Pam fancied me a little, and that alone was reason enough for her to get cracking again. None of us wanted Pam back on the game either. Pam was ready to do what the majority wished without question. She got the teas, put the music on and read her romance comics. Plotting jobs did not interest her at all.

Over the next few days I found the three a bed-sit, supplied false references and provided bedding, pots and pans and food taken from my parents. Pam was really happy with the bed-sit although she thought it was 'bleedin filthy' and was convinced that someone had died in the bed she shared with Nicky. Pam cleaned, pottered and bought bits and pieces to make it homely. It was Pam who remembered that they had to check in with a probation officer to inform her of their whereabouts. She was thrilled that they had an address at all, but felt that it would not be real unless the probation officer knew that they were settled. Chris and Nicky left to inform the authorities of their address and we 'cased joints' to burgle at the same time.

We had a great time for a couple of weeks tearing around in my Father's car and spending what money we could raise without Pam doing business. We hung out in the pubs where the marines left us alone, at the fair riding the dodgems and, mostly, in Dot's listening to music and planning. I took a day's takings to the dogs instead of to the bank and we lost the lot in less than an hour. We decided that the race-tracks were not all that 'The Rat' had cracked them up to be and we worked in detail on the job we were to execute.

Mrs. King was a friend of my Mother and owned a small but busy newsagents and tobacconists. Some weeks previously there had been an attempted break-in. It was the talk of the area for a few days and I, like the other customers, examined the reason why the thieves had been defeated. A narrow iron bar on the inside of the back-door window was screwed tight. This may have proved too much for The Grass, but I thought that it was a 'doddle' and told the others that this was the one. Never having entered King's they took the details on trust and we made preparations. Three duffle bags, a scarf for Chris, a screwdriver and gloves.

On the night we met at eleven. This was a good time for two reasons. The local Bill would be coping with the pub fights and it was not late enough to look suspicious. Next to King's was a used-car lot. Pam was briefed to be 'lookout' and either to whistle or to join us if anything untoward happened. We set off behind the shop in high excitement. Chris knew a professional way to break the window. She wrapped the scarf round and round her elbow, turned her back to the glass, centred her elbow on the middle of the pane and gave her clenched fist a hard sharp push. Sure enough the glass cracked straight up the middle almost noiselessly into two neat pieces. I was impressed. Chris pulled away each half of the glass separately — the putty was still soft from repairing the previous felons' damage and this made the job easier. Chris laid the glass quietly down. I had the screwdriver and began unscrewing the bar. Nicky caught the bar before it banged against the door (we only needed to unscrew the one end) and we stood back to examine our entrance. It was then that I realized why The Grass had given up — the space had probably been too narrow for him. But I was thin and thought that I could just make it. Chris and Nicky tried to give me a bunk-up and I tried to hoist myself through by holding onto the edge of the doorframe. I could not get enough of a hold with my fingertips and did not fancy the other two lifting me through like a corpse. So I told them that I could do it another way. Just as I was preparing to enter head first, Pam came running up. She hated being lookout it was scarey, she said; anything could happen to her standing there like that. Already two men had approached her and had not taken kindly to her insistence that she was not there for business. In the light of this unforeseen complication, we all decided to do without a lookout. Poor Pam was so scared that Nicky had to give her a hug to quieten her. The hug saved the tears that were on the way and I tried to make her laugh. I leant into the gap as far as I could and then did a forward roll into the shop. As I had hoped, Pam thought this was great. A right clown I was. Nicky was peeved and told me to stop fooling around and reminded me that we were doing a fucking job not having a P.T. lesson!

I opened the door to let the others in and we stalked about in the dark filling our duffle bags with cigarettes. When Chris told us only to take the dear cigarettes as she headed for the till, I was kite high. Chris was pleased to find the float there and wondered if there might be more money anywhere. I told her that I thought that they probably banked the takings. She did not really care what was there and neither did I; we were in and doing and that was the main thing.

After a few minutes Pam heard footsteps outside the front door and we all lay flat on the floor as Chris had instructed. A policeman doing his nightly rounds rattled the door, his torchlight passing over our flattened bodies. The policeman turned around in the doorway and seemed to get ready to move on, but then he changed his mind and stayed. Pam thought that he was going to come in until I told her that he had no keys. Then Nicky told us that he was having a fag. Pam giggled: 'Tell him we've got one he can have', and we all rolled up with laughter. Shaking and spluttering and sshhing and giggling went on until the policeman had gone.

It was hard to calm down and be serious afterwards. The mood was still with us. Pam was looking around the shop and had picked up a card in front of a huge Easter egg which was on show in King's before being donated to a local hospital. Pam informed us all that she was having the egg for her Mum. Nicky was outraged at this unprofessional suggestion and shouted that Pam could not walk along the street with that bloody great thing or we would all get nicked. But Pam was not moved, she was having it . . . she never gave her Mum nothing, not even the time of day, and there was no more to be said. When Nicky and Pam had an argument you knew that it would be a lengthy and noisy business. Chris and I agreed that it was better that Pam had the egg than take the risk of a full-blast row in the middle of a shop we were burgling. Nicky eventually agreed and Pam hid the egg under her coat as we set off along the river Exe to the car. We were jubilant, shouting to Pam that she looked pregnant and that the lorry driver could not have been such a three W's after all. But Pam was moody. As we arrived at the car and I was opening the boot to store the duffle bags, Pam shouted for us to look. She threw the huge egg into the river, rhetorically asking us, 'What'd I want to give it to her for? Never gave me nothing'. We watched the egg bobbing up and down in the river, all agreeing that whatever else Pam was she was certainly, and no doubt about it, a right nutter. We all jumped into the car, thought no more about the egg or the possibility of capture and headed for Dot's where we shelled out the cigarettes, telling everyone what we had done in detail. Dot had the good sense to refuse our offer of half price fags to sell, but she gave us free teas in celebration.

That night I stayed with the others in the bed-sit and after everyone had gone to sleep I nipped to the toilet and penned a bad poem. Most of it goes unremembered, but the last two lines stayed and reveal my feeling at the time:

I've broken your laws and entered my freedom.
I'm in front, I'm out there and I'm all on my own.

The title of the poem was, of course, 'Breaking and Entering'. Exactly what I was charged with the next day.

I wanted to go down with my mates. We had all stayed loyal and strong under questioning. I knew the score from endless conversations on the subject of arrest. You stayed silent and denied everything, never made a statement unless it was 'bang to rights' and would, most likely, get the 'hot and cold' from the Bill. Sure enough, I got the 'fatherly' concerned detective and the hard and nasty one. A third asked me if we had taken any lighters because he would like one for his wife's birthday present. (If I had known the Bill as well then as I did later, I might have supplied it!.) Yet another policeman told me that he knew we had burgled the Music Shop and where were the saxaphones? But I was not fooled by any of this. Fully briefed by all those conversations in Dot's, I was struck by the consistent recurrence of the reactions I had been told to expect. The police were not violent, although I had expected that too. I was far too naïve to realize that my 'respectable' background was my protection. Indeed, my respectable Father was on his way to the station with the best brief he could find.

I did not make the barrister's job easy. I refused bail. I did not want probation, nor did I fancy the idea of mitigation. I pleaded guilty along with my friends, so the police had not needed to push. All I wanted to do was to go to Borstal or Holloway near the Borstal Recall Wing and serve my time along with my sister villains. I had joined the criminal sorority and certainly did not want any preferential treatment. I wanted no part of the straight world anymore. Its respectability and boredom was not for me. The thought of 'getting off' and staying in Exeter to work for my Father filled me with dread. I had intentionally put myself beyond the pale — I did not want the pale dragging me back inside. Anyway, Camus had written that 'in every act of rebellion one is being true to a part of oneself'. Chris, Nicky and Pam were that part of myself that had been denied since childhood. I was and had always been an 'outsider' and I liked it that way.

I was not sent to Borstal. At the time some psychiatrist or other told me that this was due to my high I.Q. It was explained that I would corrupt the other Borstal girls — or was it that they would corrupt me? Whichever, I preferred to believe the former. That intelligence or corruptibility can be gauged by the time one takes to fit triangles into triangular shapes struck me as palpable nonsense and confirmed my belief that most people who were still inside the pale would believe anything!

Troubled Mind

I missed my three friends terribly. They had been the first women I had met who were self-defined and did not take any truck from anyone. I had been used to women who talked of nothing but Twink perms, their husbands or boyfriends, or some awful crooner or other. Where I had come from women did not drive cars and, worse, sat happily in the back whilst men sat in the front. Women did not 'talk' (because men did not listen) — they 'gossiped'. There was no politics, no larger questions, nothing beyond female trivia — all-pervading, mind-numbing trivia. Once Nicky and Chris and Pam had gone, conventional women drove me crazy. I wanted to shake them for being so complacent, so content with their second-class status. In relation to the women around me I was out on a limb and I felt it. But I wanted no part of all the compromising acquiescence these people called 'living'. I had tasted real freedom and I wanted more of it — the laughs, the highs, the vivid, the fears, the chase, the capture, the *real*. I identified with outsiders all the way. My straight acquaintances had become wet, pale, drippy and old with thinking about salaries, marriages, kids and keeping up. From what I had seen of it, I could not imagine why anyone would want to be any part of the social order.

I joined the Youth Campaign for Nuclear Disarmament (YCND). It was a foolish move, but at least these people were a minority and had something they seemed to care passionately about. I walked on an Aldermaston march, soaked my feet in the fountains at Trafalgar Square and thought that the Young Communists from Manchester were spunky. It was fine until the sit-down outside the Ministry of Defence in protest at America fronting the Cuban coup. Until that time my fellow CNDers had seemed just about alright. I had thought that they were still a bit wet and that too many were Folkniks who liked songs about earning fourpence a day or working down the coal mines. For me the trouble with these songs was that they were sung by bearded university lecturers who drank the strongest ale and earned a grand a year. But, none the less, I handled the pretension because at least this lot stuck their necks out and were civilly disobedient over something. But the sit-down at the MoD spoiled all that. Over the road, in Whitehall I suppose, was a bunch of crazies called Empire Loyalists. These precursors of the National Front crazies shouted continuous abuse at us. That was fine. I bawled abuse back at them and noticed a few odd looks from my CND friends, but I did not care. Then one of the crazies came over and landed a hard kick on my shin. Pacifism to the wind, I jumped up and kicked him hard in a place above the shins — a kick that bent him double. When more men came over there was the chance of the real set-to I was ready for. But the police surrounded us and defused it all. The Empire Loyalists looked as visibly relieved as the CNDers. I was neither relieved nor pleased. Too many of those thumb-in-the-back teachers when I was too young, or too daft, to retaliate had ensured that no one was going to kick me without paying for it. At the very least they would know that they did not take liberties with this one, even if I could not hurt them back sufficiently to beat them.

Clearly no pacifist, I realized that my days with CND were numbered. I did not doubt then, nor do I now, that the world was full of spoilers, crazies, power and money-freaks, fame and brain-chasers and dopes. I was not one who was going to sit back and let them spill their grubby minds, or kicks, over me. I left the group and headed for St Ives where, from what I had heard, the Beatniks had got it worked out and were declining altogether a part in the social mix.

Intending to sleep under the stars I had neither reckoned with the trials of sand perpetually getting in everywhere, nor could I cope with being dirty. I got a job, and therefore removed myself from the inner sanctum of the Beats, as a kitchen-hand in a cafe on the harbour front. It was hard work which I liked. I enjoyed stealing the food and shunting it out to friends on the beach who were really defying all the conventions. Crab and clotted cream, beef and pears were proudly dispensed to the dispossessed on the sands. This bunch must have been the best-fed Beats in England.

A good summer passed and I picked up with a postgraduate student from Bristol. It was taken as read that I would return to Bristol with her when the vacation was up.

Bristol was horrible. The war had gutted its heart and past. Being neither a major capital, nor a small town, Bristol was a neat place to be nowhere in. I wanted to return to London, but as Jan was taking her PhD I stayed put. Jan was well-off and had an allowance from her family, but I was not going to live off anybody and was bored of talking to student politicos and avoiding Folkniks again. There was, at that time, a cultural group called Centre 42. It had something to do with Arnold Wesker and I ran with them a bit. The idea was to take culture to the masses. (I am probably doing this group an injustice but that's how I remember it.) One night I went to a pub with them to find that the ubiquitous bearded and ale-drinking lecturers were at it again. I stood at the back of the public bar and registered the expressions of the domino-playing locals. Poetry and madrigals were hitting the air all around them. Their faces revealed a tolerant bemusement and annoyance at being patronized in this way. I burned with embarrassment at the insensitivity of the middle-class culture jerks and went home.

Fed up, I hung around the docks where people just got on with it. I took delivery of a grenade-shaped double T-shirt packed in with squares of good, black dope. I sold it to a student dealer — and made nothing as I had got the weight wrong. But I was active breezy and alive once more. I produced half-crowns, known as 'dupes', from solder, flux, plaster of paris, a matchbox and patience. It took some time before I'd perfected the art, but when I had they worked well. I weighed them against the real thing (I was not going to make the same mistake twice!) and with the centre hollowed out they slipped easily into cigarette machines. I moved around Bristol at night emptying all the machines that I could find of both cigarettes and about ten pence change. It was a fair living; I sold the cigarettes at the docks and I kept the change. There were problems of rarely having anything to spend but sixpences and coppers, but I told Jan and her friends that I made my living at illicit poker games in a dockland pub. They believed it and, in time, so did I. The gambler image and the secret life kept me perky for a while, but I still knew that Bristol was nowhere. I wanted to get to London and make it there.

Jan bought her shoes by cheque. I watched the operation closely. A few written lines, no identification . . . all you needed was the book. I asked Winston-who-got-things-for-people if there was any chance of him getting hold of cheque-books. He thought not but said that he would ask around. A few days later he called me to say that they were easy to get hold of from the ships' stewards. But, no matter what the drink for him, he was not going to collect them, no way and forget it. The stewards were all 'queers' and there was no chance of Winston being seen around the place with queers. He had his reputation to think of. I told him that by his reckoning I was queer too. That was different he said, it was no problem with girls — men were so horrible you could understand it. But men, irons (hoofs-poofs), queers . . . not a chance, forget it, no way etc. etc. I took a telephone number, arranged a meet and picked up two cheque-books for four pounds in a gay pub in Clifton.

Having learned from Nicky and Chris that you never messed on your own doorstep I had, at last, my excuse for getting back to London.

Currys . . . tape recorders. Clarkes . . . shoes. H. M. Samuel . . . gold chains. I was off. Winston put me in touch with a fence who supplied the markets. He bought at half price (above usual villain rates) and advised me what to go after. 'Don't get no radios or recorders, they've got numbers.' Sheets, crystal, shoes and more shoes, saucepans, general household — I kept the fence supplied and worked like a fiend.

I needed a car . . . worked non-stop for a week and bought one. I needed a flat . . . worked two days and rented a good one. I needed good clothes to work in and I bought, not kited, them. My own doorstep was clear and my ordinary life was quite separate from my work. I did not want anything hot on or around me. I had more than enough money to do what I wanted, although I really only wanted the life. I stopped pretending to Jan that I was some sort of maverick in a poker game. She was mortified. I was sure to get nicked and if I got nicked I would be taken away from her. I told her that I did not care about getting nicked — 'if you can't do the time, don't do the crime' — but I certainly did love her. How could I love her if I did not care about being taken away from her? I did not understand the question. Getting nicked was an occupational hazard. I did love her, but I did not care if they nicked me, that was all.

Poor Jan was talking to an assortment of B-Movie roles. I did not have the self-awareness to explain that no matter how much I cared for her, I cared more for remaining an 'outsider'. I loved the excitement of villainy, the highs, the buzz; the absolute thrill of avoiding the cloying norm that, to me, boded some kind of death knell. I was only alive when taking chances along with the others who lived that way as well. We were an élite who were not answerable to anyone for anything ever. We were the real heroes, the strong who did not swallow the nonsense, the last ones to buck the system by not only being no part of it, but also by taking it on.

Less than a year later I was arrested in rather unheroic circumstances. Returning from London with the goods stashed, I decided to check out some friends who were forming a band and should be jamming through the night. I entered a front room which smelled like a dead pub to find assorted tins of pheasant, bottles of Crème de Menthe and strange packets of foreign biscuits surrounding five very sick friends. Earlier that night the bass player, Frank, had suggested to the group that, as they were hungry and Capitalism sucked, they should go and bust open the upmarket deli down the road. And they had. Frank looked like a candidate for the nearest morgue when I tried to sober him up. With groans and rolling eyeballs all around, I decided that the most useful thing I could do was to get rid of the evidence, which some bright villain had thrown out of the window. I crept into the garden and collected tins and wrappings. Bottles were stuck in the rose-bushes and there was half a York ham on the lawn. I extricated, gathered and plastic-bagged the lot. The coal house was down in the basement. I shunted back and forth taking the evidence down and burying it under the anthracite.

I heard loud noises upstairs. Boots and whistles and Bill everywhere. I held on to my shovel, convinced that they would never take me alive, and I shot up the stairs. The Bill must have registered a figure flying out the door. I dropped the shovel and started running — I had been the hundred yards champion at one school — with nowhere to run but up the main street. Soon I was running with a Morris Minor at my shoulder! The police stayed with me at ten miles an hour until I dropped, and I soon did! I struggled a bit as they plomped me into the car, but I was too exhausted to offer much resistance. I was covered in coal dust and decidedly put out that the Bristol Bill had nothing better to chase villains with than a Wally Minor.

It was a different story at the police-station. The Detective Constable whose job it was to extract a statement from me, and who preferred to get it like teeth, got a shock when I informed him that he had better put me down because I was a woman. He had got the gender wrong. He dropped me like a stone and backed off. A WPC was sent in to confirm the worst; I would not remove my trousers. A medico was sent in; I dropped my trousers. They all wanted me gone by now and peered into my cell as if I was something from another world. My eye was blackening under the coal dust and I was making sure my nose continued to bleed. They did not like it one bit. Even provincial filth like these do not like beating up women, particularly ones with a trace of a middle-class accent between the criminal jargon. I was on my way out, unheroically bowed and bloody, when one of my friends told them that I was a kiter, where I lived and where the gear was. At the same time my record was received from Exeter.

I got six months for, the Beak said, some psychiatric treatment. A *good* result. At last I was on my way to Holloway where I belonged. A probation officer (was her name Wellbeloved?) came to my cell and cried at the sentence. My Father had told the court that I had always loved animals and was not a bad girl really, it was just the company I kept. Some silly social worker had told my Father that the responsibility for my condition was his. Girls must not be brought up as boys, even if, like him, you had six daughters and lost your only son when he was eight. But I put his mind at rest. I would not be any other way I was not a bad surrogate was I? Leave it out Dad. Made him laugh. And what was he doing coming to the court smelling like an old soak? (His brandy flask had leaked on the journey!) And anyway hadn't he burned out a ship in the dockyard when he had been thrown out of Dartmouth College for splatting a Commander with an ink-blobbed missile? Wasn't he known as 'Scrapper' throughout Plymouth when he was a kid? A chip off the old block, right? He knew it anyway and took vicarious pleasure in my misdeeds. 'Yes, but why don't you pop off the Queen and her cronies? Get rid of those privileged parasites on the backs of the good people. Do something really worthwhile?' Maybe I would one day. See you Dad.

The six months soon passed. I had had a half an hour shrink session with a Dr. De Ville during my sentence and then I was out. Disregarding prison mythology I turned back to look at all the faces around the mouths shouting 'Don't look back'. I shook my head when they shouted, 'Have you eaten your porridge?'. I would surely return to finish another bowl. That prison had not finished with me, nor I with it.

I had learned the foulest of lessons during those first few months in Holloway and all of them from the screws. I had watched them

50699

as they had bullied defenceless, simple girls who ran after them as if they were some kind of demon Mothers. I had whispered, 'Lockhand will get you in the end', as I had put on them my curse that a form of arthritis peculiar to screws would close up the hands that were forever locking doors on us. I had met women in there whose crimes were, for the most part, poverty and ignorance. But their ignorance was nothing compared to the ignorance of the screws: some were ex-army women, dragon closet-lesbians who would put you on report for hugging another woman if the mood took them; others took pleasure in winding-up the volatile knowing that they would be put 'behind the door', lose their precious smokes and, maybe, even their remission. They were cunning, ignorant, brutal and scared half-women, trapped within their fear that the buff wage-packet was not going to come anymore. Women who pleaded that they were 'only doing their job'. Screws who treated all prisoners as if they were some kind of sub-species, but were jealous of them really because they knew that, whilst we were alive they themselves were as dead to humaneness as their job decreed. I hated them. They were cruel, mocking, loathsome, abnormal, deferential, conformist half-wits. I was determined to get my own back on them for what I had seen them do to the most simple, weakest prisoners. I may have been difficult before entering Holloway, but I had not been vile; it was in there, on my first sentence, that I first learned that women as vile as screws existed. This lot left the thumb-in-the-back teachers light-years away. It was a lesson I could not forget and it inspired a hatred for those women that returns to me still.

Trouble More Or Less

In addition to my first lesson on hatred, I learned that if you bought a certain brand of tobacco the wax paper wrapping had other uses. With this wax paper newly-impressed post-office stampings could be lifted from one post-office book and inserted into another. I opened an account in a false name and tested the theory. It was empirically sound. In deference to parental wishes I went home for a week, although I knew that I would soon be off again. My friend Terry was due out in a few months and my working brief was to obtain a van and some capital. We were going into straight business selling soft toys to the innumerable hustlers

Terry knew and who, she assured me, all loved giant Teddy Bears and Pandas.

I travelled to Scotland in a tiny Fiat which exploded in Inverness. I had with me five or six post-office books in which I had entered large amounts and validated them with the wax impressions. It worked well, despite the fact that there was a waiting period between each withdrawal. I took a small cottage beside a loch as a base from which to work Scotland. Attempts at serious prose and poetry and trips to Post Offices kept me busy. I soon had the money we needed and set off back to London to await Terry's release. I met her in a newish mini van, with some hundred notes to give her a good time. I had taken a small flat for her in Bayswater in case she needed a place to stay, although I stayed in hotels because the anonymity suited my fugitive status. I also had no idea how to cook or keep any kind of home together. My Scottish sojourn had been wasted because I had eaten from tins or in restaurants and had taken all my clothes to the laundry next door to the one post office that I never used.

Terry did not want the flat and it soon became evident that she was not much into making a go of straight business either. Terry had not told me that her profession was, in fact, poncing. She knew all the hustlers alright — they were on the game for her! We went to The Fiesta in Notting Hill Gate where Terry introduced me to some women who, she told them, were working for me now . . . right! The three women seemed quite happy with the arrangement, whilst Terry was acting as if she were my benefactor. I was not happy at all. First, I told Terry that I was not, and had never wanted to be, a ponce. Second, that I thought all ponces were nonces; that I made my own money and that I could chase an earner better than most. Third, that I did not need any women keeping me thank you very much and that outside in the van were two dozen assorted Giant Teddy Bears and Pandas wholesale and were we going into straight business or fucking what? The answer was a familiar one. I was off a banana boat, came down with the last rainfall and was nobody's butch on anyone's description. I jumped on Terry just to make sure that, banana boat or not, I was not going to take this crap from anyone. Beat her too.

I carried on kiting and doing the post-office books. I was a bit miserable about Terry because we had been best mates inside. But I was glad to be no part of the poncing scene. Not in any moral sense, but because poncing was not real villainy and I was still determined to break into real crime, not play around on its periphery.

My parents moved and I felt a bit lonely so I popped down to see them. Babs was working for my parents. She was a riveting beauty and funny with it. Her presence induced me to stay around for a while and soon we were clam-close. It was me and Babs against the world and as everyone was against our friendship we left for Torquay. I took a job working for two pleasant dykes who ran a cafe and I went straight for almost a year. Jan had been right when she had claimed that I did not care much for her because I certainly did not risk separation from Babs. But the closeness was too intense for both of us. We were too young and headstrong and we parted before we ended up murdering each other — it came close to that at times.

I met another woman, middle class again, a teacher and definitely a 'good girl'. We took a cottage on Dartmoor where I walked the Tors, attempted serious prose and poetry and turned off to everything. Bored, and running out of aphorisms, I agreed to move to Plymouth in all its ghastliness. I had a reputation in the town and the introspective ego-loss of the cottage period was hanging around. Thus, when invited to meet the 'King' of the Mods who wished, so I was told, to 'do a little job', I was there faster than you could whistle Wordsworth. Over the kitchen table we worked out the details. I arranged a good alibi because I did not much trust one of the participants, though I could not refuse the offer of an 'in' without losing face.

I was decoy one and 'wheel', and I pulled into the garage as arranged. I asked the attendant for some oil and pulled up the bonnet. Mike flew into the kiosk and opened the till. The attendant heard the 'ting', looked up and rushed towards the kiosk. Mike pulled a gun on him (a toy gun I learned later). This was all too much for the attendant. He ran freaking into the road and was almost killed by a Mark 10 Jag. D--- (decoy two) pulled onto the forecourt as planned and, (dope), stayed there. I took off, picking up Mike as he ran down the street. I took him home and returned to my alibi dinner with the posh daughter of the local newspaper editor. End of story, I thought. Not so. The dopey D--- (the one I hadn't trusted), was questioned by the police when they arrived at the garage. He did not convince them of his 'just needing petrol' status. Worse, this character had collected my road fund licence for me some days before and his name was on the form. I was nicked. In the cells again I refused to admit to all the garage jobs within a hundred mile radius, even if the police *were* going to oppose bail if I did not do so. I told them to shove it and called them back and forwards to my cell to give them the names of the other gang members (they were, in fact, already in the cells but the police thought that there were more of us) who were, according to me, Batman, Robin, Carol Marx and Right Charley Windsor. I was lucky not to get beaten up before my Father arrived. A good brief followed and a charge of attempted robbery. 'Attempted' because Mike had not touched any of the money in the till. When asked by the Beak why this was so, Mike replied that he did not take it because he could not divide seven-and-sixpence into four. This witty riposte ensured that Mike received Borstal training and, as I was falling about in the dock, I received six months. The other two (laughless) gang members got off. Another wee six months did not bother me. Mike and I squeezed hands in solidarity. I was looking forward to meeting my prison friends again.

Troubled Time

Fresh into Holloway I had not counted on a six-week allocation period, locked up on an empty wing for twenty-three hours a day. Boredom scratched away at my sanity and I became increasingly obsessed with what might have happened to the petrol attendant. As in the cubicle in Tottenham Court Road, when I serioused on Trudy's heroin addiction, I could not now get the thought from my head that the garage attendant might have died through our, or rather my, stupidity. It was not just that the police had threatened to charge us with attempted murder . . . although I did think of Derek Bentley getting hanged for Christopher Craig's shooting and simple-minded Timothy Evans carrying the rope for Christie. It was that I might have been responsible for that man dying. I could not handle it at all and I swore that I would never work with other villains again. Not, you note, that I would abandon my criminal career, but that from now on I alone would determine what form my criminal activities would take. I knew that I had only gone on that job to keep up, to be 'one of the boys', to take care of my reputation. Six weeks in isolation can seem like months;

six weeks with horrors like I had can seem like six years. I re-read the gloomy Russians again and peered into *Crime and Punishment* with a jaundiced eye.

No Trouble

My sentence was uneventful. I met some nice women and on my release I was as determined as ever to make it in whatever way I could, though I needed a rest in-between.

Another brief stay in Plymouth convinced me that I never wanted to see either it or its police force again. I moved to the cottage for more attempts at serious prose, but writing and walking the moors had lost their appeal and soon my loyal friend and I made tracks for London.

I worked for a week in an office in Notting Hill, just five hundred yards from our flat in Palace Court. As had been the case previously with the civil service, the job bored me witless and on the rainy Monday of my second week I walked half way to Bland's umbrella shop. The price of a brolly was a quarter of my weekly wage. I did not buy one and I did not make it to the office either. It struck me as crazy to stay both in boring work and in penury. I also had a meet coming up to pass on love and messages to a receiver friend of a prisoner still in Holloway.

The man was there when I arrived and I noted his pure villain demeanour; crocodile shoes, Longines watch, sharp turn of phrase and an ability to scoot through *The Times* crossword in minutes. I was impressed. Alan 'the man' was always ready to do a little business if one was 'game'. Game I was, and we were soon discussing ways in which I could be useful. First, I could pick up and look after a suitcase. It was as easy as that. I was to pick up the case from Chalky, not open it under any circs, keep it for a week or so, then pass it back to Alan at a time and place to be arranged. For this little favour I was to receive two-hundred pounds — or some fifty umbrellas! It was a doddle. I admit that I did take a peek into the case, but only because I had, surprisingly, a key which fitted. My 'hold' was a heap of Georgian silver. I neither looked long at it, nor touched it, thinking that my dabs were not needed on the shiny stuff.

The hold was the beginning of a long and fruitful liaison with Alan. Soon I was kiting again and he was buying the gear. Same goods as before, only of a much higher quality. I earned less, though, because Alan paid the right villains' rate — between one-third and one-half the marked price. I travelled up and down the country with a friend and we worked a few books a week. But this was an old game to me and although it was lucrative the attitudes of the stores were changing and dangers abounded. Identification was needed, eyebrows were raised at large amounts and lists of stolen cheque-books appeared. It was not as easy as before. I also had to spend some time at the Royal Automobile Club (RAC) getting International Driver's Licences for I.D. and in using them I was establishing a working pattern that could come to the attention of the Bill.

Then Alan was offered some travellers' cheques from the boys at Heathrow and suggested that we travel abroad as this would be safer than laying them in England. We picked up the travellers' cheques from the Heathrow boys along with Alan's regular weekly suitcase. Alan had an arrangement which he called his 'lucky dip'. Every week a coach driver would 'lose' a suitcase, usually the best looking among the bunch and Alan would pay him a regular score a week for it. Some weeks the case would contain little of value, at other times Alan might be seen clicking a Hasselblad camera for a couple of days before selling it. Alan was a professional and highly successful receiver; he only took the case for the fun of the dip.

Once a week, Alan and I would meet in Hyde Park at dawn when the guards were exercising their magnificent horses. Alan would leave a briefcase in the unlocked boot of his car containing anything up to a thousand pounds in used readies. This briefcase would then be collected by various members of the Flying (lying) Squad. Alan and I would sit taking the air until the unmarked car pulled up and the police picked up Alan's 'insurance'.

I was struck by the two-way traffic of the cases from the Heathrow coaches to Alan and the cases in Hyde Park from Alan to the Bill. Alan did not think it at all ironic, and pointed out that everyone was a villain in one form or another. Whether it was postage stamps from the office, or telephone calls in the office, everyone was at it. We were the only ones who conducted our villainy honestly — we put our liberty on the line for it. We were, of course, often the losers in the game because we had to carry the can. That is, we were the pretend 'baddies' even when the odds were stacked against us; the filth were out to charge us in both senses of the word and there were no 'goodies' to be found anywhere.

I was not sure that I went along with Alan's philosophy, but it did not matter. It was the sixties and I was making a pile of money, running two flats and driving a finely-tuned sports car. I had a reserved table at the best gay club in town. I also had the status and kudos of being a villain among innumerable high-flyer friends. I was having a great time ducking and diving, meets here and gambling there, acid trips, funny bunny girls, handmade shirts and Daniel Hechter suits. I had arrived, but, unlike the other obvious products of the sixties with me at Polanski's parties, my arriving was undercover and subterranean. I thought this to be much more classy.

But I was ambitious and still just a member of Alan's firm. I wanted my own game and my own firm. I also wanted to be taken seriously by the male criminal fraternity who were, if anything, even more paternalistic than their straight counterparts. I had the money and I was game enough, but I was still a woman and women were not really trusted. A fluke was to ensure that I made it into their professional world as a trusted equal in all things bar violence. I did not like violence or violent criminals. Alan knew them all, but I knew them only slightly because I avoided any close contact. I thought that they were losers anyway — what skill was there in waving a sawn-off around? And who would put themselves on offer for sentences of ten or fifteen years? I did not particularly empathize with their victims, although I still retained the vivid memory of the near-squashed garage attendant. Maybe it *was* the thought of that garage attendant that deterred me. Maybe it was because I had always loved animals. Maybe, dare I say it, it was because I was still, quintessentially, a woman. Whatever the reason, violence in any non-defensive form was definitely not for me.

The fluke occurred in Belgium. Brussels was not my favourite place to work travellers' cheques. I thought it was pedestrian, grey and stuck in the fifties. But it was in a perfumery in Brussels that I got my chance for an independent future. Alan, and most other cheque villains, laid the travellers' by buying an expensive something (perfume, Cartier lighter) in up-market shops. This clumsy method involved selling the goods obtained to foreign fences and keeping the change. There were obviously problems with both small denomination travellers' (which nobody bought) and the nuisance of dealing with French or Belgian receivers who were often grasses and who also drove a hard bargain. I disliked the waste of time, and pondered other ways of encashment. But Alan would not hear of me entering the dreaded banks and I had to comply with his wishes because he was the boss and I a mere apprentice 'worker'.

Back in the perfumery I had purchased the bottle of Chanel No. 5 and was awaiting the change from a hundred dollar travellers' cheque (around £45) when the elegant owner informed me that he did not have enough cash on hand but, pas de problem, he would cash it at the bank up the road. I told him that the bank was fermé. (Alan also insisted that I only work the cheques when the banks were ferméd.) His reply was deafening — the banks might be closed for me, but not for him. Shopkeepers had an arrangement and could pop in between 3 p.m. and 5 p.m. for just such a little problem as had arisen; sorry and bowing and excusing me please, he was gone. I checked my rear, that is, I prepared a contingency fly-off by telling the nice shop assistants that I was un peu malade and might I sit down near the door for a little air? Sarah Bernhardt could not have portrayed a little poorly better than I did in that shop because I was increasingly feeling more than poorly wondering what Belgian prisons were like and psyching myself into a hundred-yards dash at the same time. Perched on my seat I could see the owner returning with another man, but it was clear from their casual attitude that nothing was amiss. Sure enough, he entered his aromatic parlour all smiles and thank-yous and thirty-eight pounds change.

Alan was waiting at the hotel, unprepared for the new work pattern I was to present to him. He did not fancy it, banks were trouble, this new-fangled Telex thing, automatically closing doors, what was wrong with the tried and tested method? I told him exactly what was wrong with it and set off that night touring all the Bureaux de Change, logging their whereabouts ready for a morning onslaught. The following day I entered the first and in forty seconds flat received not only the full amount less commission, but also a little receipt with a map on the back pointing out where all the other branches were. I cashed some twelve grand in two days and was ready for home. Alan was reluctantly pleased with my efforts and muttered, 'Saves on expenses too'. Praise indeed!

My share of the twelve grand was less than one although I was the worker. As in the straight world, so in the criminal world; 'workers' are paid the least and management takes the lion's share. This was fine for a while, but I did begin to think about the law of averages. I could not continue working at such a rate without running out of Bureaux and banks. (The tellers' faces were as familiar as my own sisters' in six months.) I started thinking seriously about my own firm again at the same time as a girlfriend who owned a mini-cab company phoned. She needed help. Her night controller had taken off, her drivers were all cowboys who would not hear of account work or hire for reward insurance, and her day controller was fiddling the Gatwick runs. I was sure I needed a break because I had developed an ulcer and everyone knew you got ulcers from overwork. The obvious stress involved in my chosen occupation did not occur to me at all. I offered to sort out the cab company. I took over the night control, straightened and brought the cooked books up to date, talked to the day controller and the cowboys. I took on new drivers who agreed to work the accounts and insure and this put the fears into the other drivers who eventually toed the line. It was a pleasant period, but I was beyond settling into the straight life and I was still thinking about my own firm when Gary and Adrian walked in.

Carless and pennyless, these two had just returned hirsute, tanned and gentle-eyed from Morocco. I liked them immediately and offered them a car to cab in and get on their feet. Gary was a quiet Jewish man who had worked the markets, was very handsome and rather serious about life. Adrian, his close friend, was dark and sharp, public school and funny. They were a bizarre combination with a long friendship that had survived hard times, their heterosexuality and very different backgrounds.

Gary and Adrian were fun to have around. They were game and we were soon exchanging survival tactics for, as Adrian put it, 'Never wanting or having to live on five dollars a day'. I had two members for a small firm. All I had to do was get the travellers' cheques. This would not be easy; not because Alan was the 'middle man', as he did not keep both ends apart and I knew all the suppliers; but because it would be highly unethical to poach on his territory. Reputations are very important in professional villain circles; I was not about to be a poacher. I had a telephone call from the West Ken villains. I had received plenty of calls before but had always given them a blank because they were bad news on anybody's reckoning. But I needed the means to the end and although dealing with the West Kens was foul means indeed, I agreed to a meet with them. Their professionalism would be clear from their offerings on the first meet. Tens of thousands of Dexedrin in brown paper bags; a heavy brass ring and a job lot of genuine Persian carpets made of 80 per cent nylon. I told them not to waste my time. I did not deal in drugs. No, I was not aware that Bengali gold carried no hallmark, but I was not prepared to weigh it thank-you very much. And, if they must burgle carpet shops, would they kindly redirect their operations from the Mile End Road to Knightsbridge. Eventually a West Kenner did come up with some travellers' cheques which were fresh and carried a forgable signature. I paid him below the going rate because of all the time wasted on futile meets and Gary, Adrian and I set off to make our first grand.

On our return I called Alan and asked him straight out if he would be interested in selling the travellers' to me instead, of me working the things. I added that I felt I could not continue as a worker — a matter of time and all that — and that I had a couple of good 'faces' keen and ready to go to work. To my surprise Alan told me that he had been expecting it, he agreed that it was time I got going on my own, to be lucky and yes, I could buy from him at 10 per cent above the usual rate and that would be fine.

I had cracked it. I had retired as a worker and I had, at last, made my way from being just another face to running my own little firm.

No Trouble At All

Supplies of travellers' cheques came pouring in and soon Gary, Adrian and I were flying out from Heathrow three times a week, cashing up the cheques and, like all good white-collar workers, back home by five-thirty.

I felt a bit of a cheat not actually doing the encashments and putting myself on offer in the same way as the other two, but my qualms ensured that I became increasingly more wary and professional.

It was imperative to me that we created no work patterns, but as the RAC continued to supply excellent identification in the shape of International Driver's Licences complete with photograph —

without us having to supply a British licence to obtain them — we decided to use these. But I thought Gary and Adrian should have better I.D. I had heard that an Adana printing machine could handle simple printings and I noted that my driver's licence was merely a green slip stuck into a red booklet. I purchased an Adana and spent hours lining up the little silver blocks until I had perfected the firm's first driving licences.

We had been working for a while when I read an article in *The Times* about the inception of the new Eurocheque system. A banker's card would indemnify any cheque for thirty pounds at any bank in the European network. This seemed too good an opportunity to miss and I put out an order for a book and card. We soon got one — although the signature it carried was so difficult that Gary and I set to and 'cleaned' it. Oily nail-polish remover mixed with Fairy Liquid combined to make a noxious fluid which lifted the signature right off. Unfortunately, it took the plain white signature strip with it! Undeterred, we nipped to a garage and bought a spray can of Duplicolour car paint. We masking-taped the card and finely sprayed coat after coat. The end result was perfect. No more signatures to forge, no identification needed for the Eurocheque other than the card, up to nine-hundred pounds a book, a book a day easily. We thought it a fine doddle. We must be the first ones at it too!

We set off the next morning, chirpy if a little worried because this was a new game. The Eurocheque system was only a few weeks old and we did not know what safeguards the banks had built into it. We should not have worried. There were no lists of stolen books, no I.D. asked for and no problems. We whisked up the Champs Elysees and had the book cashed by elevenses. It was such a quick operation because Gary began cashing two cheques per bank, then three, then four. I told him to stop at four because we did not know what limit had been set by the banks before they checked the cheques. Gary promptly asked to cash five cheques at the next bank and was told that he could if he had his passport for identification.

Back in London, I considered the recurring problem of identification. I went to a Labour Exchange to find out what one needed to obtain another beneficial innovation — the British Visitor's Passport. I examined what identification was needed from us to get the identification we needed from them for identification!

Would you believe it? A medical card! Black printing on ordinary white card, no watermarks, no embossing. I sped back to the Adana 'print tank' that we had set up in the basement. Again I spent hours lining up and jiggling the silver blocks around. But it was no good. There was a small printed crown on the medical card and I was no artist and did not have the right equipment. I called Peter the Print. This was obviously a photo-plate job.

Two days later, and for a tenner each, I took delivery of fifty perfect, blank, black and white medical cards. I immediately put out orders for cheque-books and cards; as many as anyone could get. I raised the going price a little to make sure that we had the edge on the Home Kiter's League and waited for them to roll in. They soon did.

Gary was a terrific worker, he had bags of nerve and energy and looked and sounded the biz. Gary was, if anything, too game and I had to keep his bottle in check. Unlike Adrian, who was at least polite about his work, Gary acted so much as if the cheques were his that he laid them like an irate businessman and was thoroughly rude to the tellers. I worried that one day Gary would be too terse and get a pull because of it. But it never happened and Gary was soon number-one face in a small firm that was growing fast.

Before long there were five workers — two part timers and Dolly who came on to the firm full time. Dolly was very much a sixties woman. She was loud and attractive, funny and intelligent, although daft enough to be keeping a no-talent guitarist boyfriend. A lot of women I knew kept men who were on the periphery of the rock business. All of them were going to 'make it' the next day. Some women, like Dolly, clad themselves in Mr. Freedom gear; but most were sort of Earth Mothery — decked in floral skirts or granny dresses and sporting vegetarian babies called Sky or Space in hammocks on their backs. These women aspired to be wise and gentle in the sense that they threw the I-Ching, read the Mystics, had Gurus and discussed the relative merits of yoga and yoghurt. Their men called them their 'ladies' and were, mostly, indolent characters with weirdy beards and flowing hair. I thought these men a prideless lot because they happily ponced off their ladies and hippily ponced off the State. Criminal or no, I thought they gave the genuine needy a bad name!

I first met Dolly on a meet where she was purchasing some drugs for the no-talent boyfriend. I next saw her in Mr. Freedom and we went for a coffee. Dolly showed me some forged hundred-dollar bills she had bought and was about to lay on the London banks. I knew that these had been on offer some two years before. They were dangerous, not because they had been doing the circuit for so long, nor because the paper they were printed on was a dead buff (that was alright if the notes were made to look really old before encashment), but because the little clock on the back of the bill was bereft of hands with which to tell the American time! I advised Dolly not to lay them but she told me that things were hard. I knew how it was, the boyfriend was going to make it the next day, all he needed was a decent Gibson guitar, it was just the breaks in the business, that was all. I knew how it was alright — I had heard all this so many times. But as I was turning away cheque-books with the prefix Miss or Mrs, I told Dolly that she could join the firm on the understanding that she took no more occasional lines of heroin — erstwhile junkies we did not need.

Dolly and Adrian got on well but Dolly and Gary were competitive and tried to outdo each other by upping the amounts of cheques they laid in each bank. I put the lid on this by insisting that neither was to cash more than a hundred-and-fifty a bank because I had learnt that this was the highest amount before reaching the get-on-the-Telex maximum. It was not true, but I did not want these ego matches for number-one status getting them both captured. The lie worked well, the competitiveness eased and we all got on fine.

We were known as 'the happy firm' to other villains and it was true. We laughed at and about everything and at everyone doing their mundane thing. As I had been a worker myself and knew all the pitfalls, I took as many precautions as I could for all our protection. We had an unwritten code of rules to this end:

Rule One was that the books and cards were always fresh.
Rule Two was that we might travel together but only without knowing each other.
Rule Three covered speed of operation. We flew to where we were working, did the work, then flew home (or on) immediately.
Rule Four was that we stayed at the best hotels because they afforded the most anonymity and also put one in the right frame of mind for working.

Rule Five came later and was that if we did have to travel from one workplace to another, no one was to go out or drink the night before working and that all should be in bed at a reasonable hour.

Rule Six was that only I was to carry the works out of Heathrow and the money when we returned.

Rule Seven was that I was to destroy all the evidence (passports, cheque stubs, receipts etc) immediately after encashment.

Rule Eight covered contingency plans in the event of our arrest.

The two (then three, then four) part timers were women who worked independently but who had the odd quiet time. They, too, were excellent workers and we successfully liaised when I had more books and cards than we could handle in a given time. This subcontracting was essential to keep within Rule One — that all cheque-books must be fresh. For example, the West Kens would do a little burglary, but only sell the negotiables when they had spent all the readies. I always checked the last counterfoil on the cheque-books and would not buy the book if it was more than five days old. Now and then, knowing my policy, a villain would attempt to forge the last counterfoil by moodying the paying of a gas bill or some such thing. All that should be said about that is that maybe there is no-one easier to con than a conman, but these forgeries to a forger had as much chance of getting past me as my hand written sick notes had had of getting past a thumb-in-the-back teacher!

We worked hard, did well, and the sixties passed. Along with them went any liking I had ever had for straight life. I mixed with villains because I enjoyed their company. I also liked being in touch with what was going on in the under place. I knew who had cracked this one, chased that one, burgled that place. I knew too, who was supposedly cemented up in the Marylebone Flyover, whether the infamous so-and-so had really been murdered and how they had supposedly disposed of the body. I knew how much that landed family really had lost (or gained, if the family wealth was in trust and the 'robbery' was a set-up insurance fiddle). I took vicarious pleasure in handling, if not buying, that lovely Utrillo painting and the amazing eleven-carat diamond that was later sold over tea in Fortnum's to a household-name actress who had a penchant for fabulous, if bent, jewellery.

Villains were a lot of fun and much more generous than their straight counterparts. They were good to their extended families and friends and it was nothing for an ex-con fresh from prison to receive a couple of hundred notes in tens and twenties from the thieves who supposedly have no honour amongst them. The professional villains also had the healthiest contempt for money. Not for them the daily grind, the boss crawl or the Abbey National nest-egg. They would either chuck their earnings onto the gambling tables or buy absurdly expensive presents, meals and bottles of booze for their loved ones and friends — without being flash about it. (Only the amateurs were flash.) After all, a professional villain could make a grand again the next day if she or he felt like it.

I did not always feel like it. Heathrow Airport held all the excitement of a bus shelter. The staff treated me like the regular I was, greeting me with a 'good morning', or a 'had a good day?' on my return. The stewardesses got to know that I would arrive as late as possible to avoid the flying holidaymakers and shoot onto the plane two minutes before take-off. I carried nothing but under-seat baggage. My brief-case, containing a poster catalogue, an order book and a paperback or two, was hardly suspicious. Occasionally, for the fun, I would stroll through the red zone when I came back, absentmindedly forgetting that I had nothing to declare, or so it seemed. In fact I would be carrying between three and ten-thousand pounds in foreign readies. I changed most of the takings to Swiss francs because the Swiss sensibly print a hundred-pound note and this made my carrying less bulky. I kept a bribe roll separately from the takings because I had once, by way of a bribe, lost two grand to a customs gentleman in Le Havre. I never had the chance to learn if the Heathrow customs' men were as amenable as the French. To be fair to them, I seriously doubted it, though I would certainly have tried them out if given a pull.

Although my teacher friend and I had a great relationship, the divide between my criminal allies and my straight friends widened. Our lives were so different. I still believed that most straights were wet or docile with the life drained from them because of their conformity through fear. Strangely though, I liked the peripheral straight least of all. As in my previous dealings with the Beats, I liked the philosophy behind the hippies' rebellion, and I was pleased, too, that writers like Kerouac and Ginsberg got some long-deserved recognition. But I did not think much of the hippies themselves. Their behaviour and American terminology seemed phoney and heralded nothing to me but the satellite, banana-monarchy status that was to come in the eighties.

The Americanized hippies undermined our language. The Filth or the Bill was, to them, the Fuzz. One did not get captured or nicked anymore, one got busted. 'Boodle' and 'scratch' became 'bread' at about the same time as 'brasses' became 'hustlers' then 'hookers'. These hookers did not 'go case' anymore, they turned 'tricks' with their customer 'steamers' who were now 'punters'.

There was a clear separation of language and although I used the criminal jargon less the more professional I became I still enjoyed the rich argot of the underworld. The score, pony, monkey, long 'un, readies, scratch, tickle, boodle, hoist, kite, scam, blag, crack, Tom, fit up, verbal, graft, grass, Bill, beak, nick, boob, choky, porridge, bird. It was our language, common usage now, but exclusive to villains in the sixties and a small safeguard in the sense that only a straight, a fool or an amateur would offer a long 'un for something worth a hundred pounds.

I spent some time thinking about improving our work methods. It was simple enough. I would take delivery of the cheque-books and cards, strip and paint the cards, fill in the medical cards with the names on the cheque-books and add a four-digit number to a spurious doctor's signature on the bottom line. The workers would then take the medical card, appropriate form, two photographs and, I think, twelve-and-sixpence to the Department of Employment where they would receive a British Visitor's Passport on the spot. Time and motion studies revealed that it was less work and undangerous to spend one day obtaining four or five passports per worker. This did make for a bulkier carry out of Heathrow, but I did not mind because, as I have said, I was as familiar to the airport staff as the glosswork. Larger workloads kept expenses down too, although we did have to move on after one day's work and stay at wherever we were working the following day.

Before the creation of Rule Five put a stop to it, it was fun doing all the clubs in Paris or Berlin after we had finished in Amsterdam or Zurich. But clubbing soon palled and we preferred to stay in our hotel rooms laughing and hatching lunatic plots over room-serviced tables of crab and pots of tea. We were always glad to return home when the work was completed.

We continued to work like there was no tomorrow. Gary was affectionately known as Mr. Consumer Durable because he took pleasure in owning Nikon cameras, quadrophonic stereo outfits and the like. Adrian was something of a dope buff and would travel a thousand miles for some strong Lebanese Red or Thai stick. Dolly was still keeping her boyfriend and was generous to the generally disadvantaged; she could not pass a match seller or drunk without laying some money on him (twice as much if it was a woman). I did this, too, although it struck me initially as being nothing but bad-conscience money — and phoney for being so. I knew that most of the recipients would not have the meal or find the bed they could get with the money. But I also knew that a bottle of Scotch or sherry might keep them warm or even alive on the Strand overnight. After a while I became superstitiously convinced that if I did not look after the unders I would surely get arrested.

Another two years passed. We would fly out maybe twice or three times a week, but all of us were taking longer and longer holidays in between working, pretending it was for the fun rather than for a much-needed break from the stress. I do not remember stopping to think about what I was doing and why. I was too busy ducking and diving and buying and flying for any self-examination. I still took pleasure in my work although the routineness of it got to me at times.

The spur to self-examination came in the unlikely form of an actress who was a member of a far-left political party. The actress was a highly articulate Marxist and over the next few months we talked of nothing but *The Communist Manifesto, The German Ideology* and *Capital.* I had never read such books before and these works were revelatory. Of course, I agreed, capitalism was morally barren. Certainly we are alienated from our true being. Yes, Nature should be an egalitarian benefactress to us all and is turned against us because we have to buy her to live. Capitalism sucked! I had often said it, but I had said it unthinkingly. Now I knew why capitalism sucked. My crude analysis veered around the fact that one-eighth of us own seven-eighths of the social cake for no better reason than an accident of birth. The other seven-eighths of us are entitled to some of the remaining one-eighth, but only if we labour for it and even then our work is ripped off and goes back to the robbing one-eighth because they had invested their capital (which they had in the first place) into raw produce and our workplaces.

This had to be the long firm fraud of all time. What a rip off! I seethed. Here was I doing my thing with nary a victim in sight other than the ledgers in the banks. Here was I risking my liberty without taking anything like the liberties of the capitalist entrepreneurs who did not risk going down at all. Not even if they stole two-thirds of a miner's lungs for their dividends! Not even if they starved out the tea workers who pick the very stuff these ghouls turn into money! These people, who bet at their own bookies on whether more or less of us are going to buy the stuff that we produce and then invest or strip accordingly, actually had the nerve to argue that workers who go on strike for more pay are holding the country to ransom. Ransom indeed! What greater ransoming can there be than selling one's own country's money when it weakens against other currencies — and thereby weakening it even further. This lot do that at their bookies too. Can you believe it? Nor could I. Even my superficial analysis threw up the villains in the pile. The actress had a convert. And the Stock Exchange might well have had a bombing if I had known where to get hold of a bomb!

I carried on working with a vengeance, I donated money to the party and this time it did not feel like bad-conscience money at all. But, over time, my revolutionary fervour and revelatory beliefs dissipated in the light of my daily activities. I was still staying in five-star hotels because of the anonymity they provided and in them I was close to the evil capitalists. Fat Americans, elegant English homosexuals and square-headed businessmen who bored everyone to death. Despite their Gucci shoes, their wives were still candidates for the chiropodist whilst the flash new rich were still bemused by their own gold Rolex when it slipped from under the cuff. It was hard to pin a conspiracy of malice onto this miserable ulcered bunch. The more I thought about the supposed plight of the working classes the less sense it all made. How come they did not get together if they were being ripped off all the time? Why didn't they drop tools, force the thieves out of business and stop putting bricks one on top of another for houses that they would never be able to afford to buy? And why should I support a group who, like their masters, picked on Asians, Blacks, Gays and women? I asked my actress friend if these working classes were worth fighting for? Surely they should be able to see who was robbing them and then do something about it? Instead, they doffed their caps and bent their knees. Certainly the capitalists keep the greater spoils, but the working classes shore up the system by their acquiescence. I left the Party.

The excitement was going from villainy. I was bored with flying all the time. I never wanted to see another George V or Hilton. People in general disgusted me to a greater or lesser degree. The money piled up, but for what? I decided that I needed a long break away from villains, straights and politicos and I took off to Morocco with Goethe and Nietzsche to dispel the ghosts of Engels and Marx. The latter were certain to be insipid besides this duo, or so I thought. I settled into Mogador, a fishing village in the South of Morocco, and I got my head down.

Inner Trouble

I tried to convince myself that I was suffering from a temporary malaise caused by the routine nature of my work. But I knew that this could not be true because, at the same time as I was lying angstfully in the sun, two post-graduate students at the Royal College of Art were engaged in perfecting the photo-plates for our own cheque-books. I had been considering forgery again and a cheque-book was hardly a bank-note. Sure enough, the process was a simple one. The production of the banker's cards was more difficult. But Frank had put me onto Benny, who knew all that there was to know about the possibilities of plastic. I had telephoned Benny before I had left and he had told me that there was only a minor stage to go before our requirement was met. Benny also knew a perforator who was due out soon. It was a nuisance to have one's cheque-book stolen and there would be no victim at all if we could make our own works.

Normally I would have delighted in these steps to self-sufficiency. But something was wrong — although I did not know what. In Morocco I had the time if not the will for some much-needed self-examination. I had got all that I had thought I wanted; money, success and credibility with professional male villains. But why I had wanted it quite so much was not clear at all. For sure, villains were apparently the furthest removed from the social set-up, but they had their own set-up too which in essence was not that different.

I nipped in thought to my childhood, hoping that I might summon a theory or two as to why I was feeling so out on a limb again. I remembered occasional traumas like being forced into a dress once — a single tube on my two legs. I had been appalled! Not only had it been impossible to climb, but this single tube, had not covered a part that was not to be seen and boys could look up it if one was up trees. But most girls leave behind the coercions of a female childhood, so the dress episode could hardly provide reason enough for going to the lengths I had gone in order to escape from all things feminine. I was a rational adult now and I had no great opinion of formative-years theory. It was true that to me being 'feminine' was all that was lowest and most servile. To be feminine was to cheat, to sell oneself by creeping around seeking the attention of men to keep you. No grown woman could really enjoy being a frippy dependent. I believed that I had respect from men and not just from wet straight men either. It was the same respect that had been afforded Nicky and Chris all those years before because they had given and taken it 'like a man'. This was surely a rational response to all those who are still only too willing to follow Henry VIII's contention that women can most properly be classed alongside lunatics and children! How many times had I heard in childhood that our brains were smaller than men's! It had worried me so much at the time that I read books on the subject and told my Father that unless he thought prehistoric man brighter than modern man his theory was up the creek because Neanderthal man's brain was heavier than ours. It was, of course, useless to argue. My Father, along with most men, did not even need to argue, women just *were* inferior and that was that.

I knew that trying to find the woman I was had something to do with the malaise, but at that time I could not separate being a woman from being a 'feminine' woman and there were no Greers or Millets around either. The time had not come when women would make a political choice to lesbianism and turn their backs on those precursors of modern feminism, the 'tomboys'. In fact, later, some feminists were cruelly and crudely to accuse me, and all the other women who had refused to take on the feminine role, of being male emulators.

Whether I was emulating the oppressor or not, my one-time

admiration for guts, nerve, ingenuity and street wisdom now deserted me. I was just another criminal. I had no beliefs about anything, nor did I admire or respect anyone, apart from a few long-dead writers and poets. How I had managed to live for so long without meeting some group or some belief to hold on to I did not know.

I sat for hours every day watching dung beetles carrying their dinners up the sides of sand dunes. Normally I would have found some humour in the situation, particularly as some of the beetles would lose their cargo just before reaching the top of the hill. I tried to summon a mock pretentious laugh at their Sisyphean labours, but the never-ending futility of their work mirrored my life so closely that I could not. I thought that I had nowhere to go but back to crime which would mean that I would go back to prison. The thought of prison steeled me and I put on some mental bravado. I determined that, no matter what, I would give them (and 'them' was everyone but villain) a run for their sentence.

The depression eased a little and after a few months, acclimatized from a few days in Switzerland, I returned home.

The perforator had got another sentence and would not be out for some time, so we carried on as before. My motivation was lessening each day and I got my only criminal interest from examining other ways of working on long firm fraud and letters of credit. Long firm fraud was simply the setting up of a bona fide business, undercutting all the competition, paying the bills initially to build up one's credit worthiness, then ordering a mile of gear (coal, general goods, etc.) selling it all and taking off. Not much brain needed for a long firm, just patience and capital. I did not fancy it. Letters of credit had something to do with depositing a large amount in a set-up bank account then travelling abroad with the letters for large amounts, cashing them over and over until the bank got used to you and trusted you. Then you withdrew nearly all the money in the English account at the same time as a suitable identified person withdrew it abroad. I did not fancy this much either as all one was doing was doubling up. Still they were new games and something to think about.

I popped over to Morocco quite often to have what I saw as my think stint but the more I thought about the future the deeper the returning malaise.

Ironically, I had attempted to ease myself from the firm and give it over to the part-time and full-time staff of eight. Adrian was the only member of the firm who was ready to go it alone and he took on a little run with Alan 'the man'. But they broke our Rule Two and travelled out of England together. They were arrested — though the charges were overlooked at a cost of a few hundred to the Bill. Adrian's arrest put the fears into the other members. They thought that the firm would be jinxed if I pulled out (we were very superstitious). I did not bother much, thinking that I might just as well carry on with it as do anything else. I should have realized when the depression returned that an angstful villain overlooks danger signals.

Dead Trouble

I registered the red Hillman watching us on the New Kings Road and thought no more about it. I picked up the three books and cards, thanked and paid the supplier and drove to the passport office where I was to liaise with Dolly. Driving home I noticed the same red Hillman behind us and, again, I did nothing. I can hardly explain this. I saw them and yet I did not see them. I knew that it was the police and yet I did not know. I certainly did not consider that they might be about to capture us when they had been after us for years and I had just watched them observing me on a meet!

Ten minutes later my flat was full of Flying Squad including one WPC Saint. I mention Ms. Saint because if she had not been present I could have bought the lads off and that would have been that. I am pretty sure of this because the two I approached on this matter assured me, somewhat aptly, that they were as 'sick as pigs' not to get an earner, but I knew how it was these days, what with all this clean-up the force business. I knew alright. A 10^2 had bankrupted many a Bill known to us for taking 'insurance'.

I should, I suppose, have been shocked, even horrified, at the arrest. In truth, I was simply relieved that it was all over. Gary was white with shock. Dolly poured, and was about to sip, a little whisky when Ms. Saint took it from her. But Dolly remained perky and told the assembled that at last she would now have the time to study yoga seriously.

I was pleased that Dolly was behaving with front and style, but I thought it odd that here I was in a situation where I could go down for five years and yet feel as though five years had been lifted from me at a stroke. The malaise also lifted and I took care that we all remembered the contingency plans for arrest before being taken to the police station.

The contingency plans were very simple. We could choose either to stay silent or to make a statement but no one was to involve anyone else at any stage and was to confess only their own part. In this way the snowball-rolling conspiracy charge would not gather unnecessary captives. For example, we would have to accept that we had used medical cards because of the evidence, but Peter the Print need not be involved because I would say that I had bought them in a pub from the ubiquitous 'man in a pub'.

Dolly and I were fine at the station. Dolly was standing on her head in a cell telling various officers not to worry because she could do a sentence standing on her head. I did a Jimmy Durante when the police took our fingerprints (always a downer to the uninitiated) by placing a plastic mug on my nose and making schnozzy tunefuls as they rolled my hands back and forth on the ink-plated piano!

Before long I realized that a grass was at work. I could not think who it was but some broke or captured villain was certainly earning his thirty pieces somewhere because we were joined by two, then three, then five other members of the firm. Dolly and I confided to each other that we were feeling relieved at the arrest.

Not so a couple of the men. They were not going to be able to do the time, they were feeling sick, they wanted a solicitor and bail on the spot. They moaned like professional wailers rather than professional villains. I was embarrassed by their behaviour and felt that the Bill would have one up on us if they continued. I was about to call to them when a Bill banged on their cell door and told them to stop behaving like a bunch of women. Dolly and I were incensed at this piece of arrant sexism and told him that we had had enough of the insults. The Bill countered our call by telling the men, 'See, even the women aren't making a fuss like you lot!' Dolly and I ached with laughter at this plod's attempt at fairness between the genders.

Dolly thought that the police would permit a telephone call to a solicitor. I knew better, but our 'contingency plans for arrest' included a friend who would soon hear of our arrest and get our brief along.

The police then produced their trump card. They brought my

teacher friend to the station. She was heavily pregnant having decided some months before that she wanted a child. The deal was that if I made a statement the police would not charge my friend. As I knew that they could disinter my Grandmother and charge her with conspiracy if they so chose, I fenced around a bit. They offered their word that they would let my friend go *after* I had made a statement. I laughed. I gave them my word that I would make a statement after they had let her go. They laughed. Eventually they agreed to let her go with the proviso that if I did not come up with a confession they would arrest her again within minutes.

My friend had not been involved at any level in the firm apart from continuously telling me to give up the criminal life, but I thought it quite fair that the Bill used her for a deal in this way. I made a statement admitting to my part and the Bill kept their word.

The statement took hours. It was impossible to remember all the places that I had been to and I was concerned that even more would come to light after the trial. I did not fancy a gate arrest after finishing the one sentence and then getting another. Again the Bill stuck to their word and took into consideration all outstanding charges. I probably took on the work of other firms but I did not mind in the least. The police could increase their clear-up rate as long as I could clear up mine in one go.

Dolly asked me what I thought I would receive by way of sentence. I told her five years. We both agreed that this seemed reasonable because of the amount involved and the forged passports — also because we would be going up the steps at the Bailey.

The police told me that they would not oppose bail the next day and I talked with Dolly about whether she should stay silent or make a statement. I did not want to influence her decision but when we weighed up the evidence: two passports with her photo on; two uncashed cheque-books and cards; dabs that, so they said, they had on a processed cheque, there seemed little point in going for a not guilty. I advised Dolly to wait for the solicitor but she wanted to get it over with. Dolly called the Bill to our cell, gave me the thumbs up and went off to make her statement.

Gary also went out and made a brief statement. I called to him to wait for the solicitor (he did not know of my enforced deal), but he called back that he wanted no opposition to bail. I learned later that Gary was particularly keen to get bail because he did not intend to stick around for the trial.

The police were delighted to have the 'happy firm' under wraps and kept their word on all counts. The next day bail was granted and we all repaired to a pub to discuss briefs, sureties and the future. A couple of members wanted to continue working. I was not surprised but I was not interested either. We made arrangements to meet at the Temple to go over our defence. I did not think that there was much to go over. I certainly had no defence as such and I hated the idea of the usual psychiatric or social-factor type mitigation. I think it was Nietzsche who said that the criminal does not live up to the courage of the act when s/he pathetically throws herself on the mercy of the court. Mercy indeed! Who needs it, I asked the others? We had done it, we had known what we were doing, we had had a ball. If you can't do the time, don't do the crime, etc. But, Dolly apart, no one was convinced. They also thought that I had been acting strangely for some time because I had wanted to leave the firm to them. The court games were about to begin although it would be a year at least before the trial. It was not for any noble reason that I was against making a defence to the court — it was more that I thought it demeaning and cheap to give the supposed straights more grist for their pseudo-honest mill. I was thoroughly sick of the continuous criminal cry that it was all because of one's upbringing, or lack of education, or mental instability. We were personable, intelligent and had as much going for us as anyone. Why should we pretend to be some kind of inadequates? I refused to identify with disadvantaged losers in the social lottery. I had travelled as much as I had wanted and I had experienced more excitement than most. I had enjoyed both the dangers and the rewards and my criminality was the result of a rational choice — nobody had coerced or cajoled me into it.

The only pang of regret that I did have was that I had not given up the Eurocheque game when I had become bored with it. I should, I knew, have quit whilst I was still ahead. I also knew that my boredom had fuelled the recurring depression and that it had made me careless. Notwithstanding the grass, our arrest was really down to me.

Looking For Trouble/Trouble Found

A year or so later we appeared at the Old Bailey. In the interim I had travelled to Morocco (the police had not thought it worthwhile to keep our passports!) chasing Gary so that he could fulfil his promise to a friend of mine who had stood bail for him. When I arrived I found Gary and Adrian in a soporiphic stoned state. Both were incapable and I was dismayed to hear that they thought that because my friend was an old Etonian they were not morally obliged to repay him the money. This was a bad argument and they knew it because Mike had only stuck his neck out for them down to friendship. But bad happens as bad does and Gary and Adrian were later arrested in Spain and Mike received his bail money around the time we were preparing ourselves for some heavy sentences.

As luck would have it, our case was considered to be so complex that a special company-fraud judge was picked to sort it all out and adjudicate. This was good news for us as we could have been landed with one of the Bailey's Jeffreys.

The grass had done his work well and there were eleven of us in the dock. Peter the Print was there and Alan and his wife. (She produced a lady in a wheelchair who told the judge by way of mitigation what a fine woman Alan's wife was and how she had helped her fend off a gang of vicious louts about to mug her.) Dolly, and the firm's first part timers were also there, including the husband of one of them. The husband was something of a joke and, although he had happily reaped the benefits of his wife's work (he drove a new Mercedes), insisted that he knew nothing and no one to such a degree that he would not speak to any of us, not even to his own wife!

Alan was as gentlemanly as ever and behaved in a thoroughly professional manner. It was good to see him again, even in such unpleasant circumstances. Alan and I had a good laugh at the 'don't know anyone not even my own wife' defendent and we talked about mutual friends and politics.

The trial went on for days. I sat in the dock and grappled with *The Times* crossword. I was being neither flash nor blasé but I had seen the film and read the book and the court case was so boring that I could have fallen asleep. I was, however, prepared for the worst when we stood up to receive the familiar and just penalty for unjust desserts.

Alan was given a two-and-a-half year sentence which was a good result as he already had an outstanding two years suspended. Dolly received Borstal training which was totally out of order because this was her first offence. The two part timers received eighteen and twelve months each which was a shock as this was their first offence as well. Gary and Adrian did not show and everyone else got off with non-custodials.

I cannot remember one word the judge said to me. No doubt it was the usual stuff: 'I have no alternative but to sentence you to a period of imprisonment.' All I did hear was 'two years'.

The farce was over. The little-wigged players had done their bit and the bigger-wigged had done his. I waved goodbye to my friends in the gallery.

2
Christina: In her own Time

Diana Christina and Pat Carlen

Diana Christina's father first took her to court as being in need of care and protection at the age of fourteen. In the same year, and before she had reached the age of fifteen, she was at an Approved School. On her eighteenth birthday she was on a diet of bread and water, in solitary confinement in Exeter prison. Today, at the age of forty-seven and after spending almost a third of her adult life in gaol, Christina is both crime-free and gaol-free. Yet who is she? How did the young, comfortably-off girl educated at the French Lycée in London become the prostitute, the cat burglar, the shop-lifter, the pimp and the prison-hardened gaol-bird? Who, indeed, was the woman behind the headlines? Christina has been searching for answers to that question for the last sixteen years. In this chapter we tell two stories; the story of that search and the story of the criminal career that led up to it. Christina's story is told in her own words. Pat Carlen's commentary, structuring and interpretation of that story is informed by a sociological perspective which, in describing Christina's complex character, focuses both on the social and sexual repression of women in general and on the part it played in the making of Christina as a committed criminal in particular.

Diana[1] — Her Father's Daughter

'In my father's house we went on tippytoes.'

My two earliest memories are of stealing a scooter and of seeing a crowd of people panic themselves into a mob during an air-raid. I took the scooter from outside a shop and lied to my mother about how I'd come by it. A policeman came and

59

took it off me and I never heard any more about it. I was three years of age at the time and years later when I told my mum that I remembered the whole incident she was amazed — she had never dared to let my father know. The other experience was more traumatic and even more memorable. In my mind's eye I have this picture of being with my father in a crowded street. Suddenly he hoisted me onto his shoulders and began to run. The crowd panicked and ran in all directions. I saw people pushing each other aggressively and heard them swearing a lot. A bomb had dropped somewhere quite near to us and as I sat there looking down on the people, straight ahead of me I could also see multi-coloured flames leaping up to the sky. A riveting scene! I was three years of age. I don't know which of those two experiences came first.

Shortly after that came the evacuation. I remember very vividly that I was suddenly in a strange house and that my parents had disappeared. My mother, though born in England, was of Italian parentage. My father was of Swiss parentage, and had also been born in England. They had placed me with an Italian woman in a village in Berkshire. When I realized that my parents had disappeared I began to scream and weep. The woman gave me my big china doll as a comforter. I threw the doll down to the ground, smashing her to bits. I remember giving my baby brother the doll's head which had remained intact. I also remember other children throwing stones at me and calling out 'Dirty Eyetie'. My father and mother came to see me and my brother once a month. I was always glad to see them because they brought us presents but, after smashing my dolly, I just didn't seem to miss them any more. Night-time was terror-time for me there. I was alone in a dark room, haunted by monsters of all kinds, as well as wild animals. Every night I froze, stilled my breath and, silently as a ghost, slid to the end of the bed under the covers where I disappeared into the void of sleep until morning.

Although the woman with whom Diana was staying was not unkind to her she did not show the little girl any warmth and affection — any physical contact in the form of cuddles was completely lacking.

In such a situation it is not surprising that Diana became very attached to a kindly Italian prisoner-of-war by whom she was befriended sometime before she left Berkshire to return to her parents.

Romeo used to sit me on his lap and sing to me. He would also play the accordian. He was an Italian prisoner-of-war who came into our house towards the end of the war. I remember that when my parents came to take me back home I was on his lap, and I clung to him and screamed that I didn't want to leave him. But that was all over very quickly and it sums up the period to the end of the war.

Straight after that came Holy Communion time and the RAF man. I don't know which came first. What I do remember very vividly is going up the aisle to receive my First Holy Communion in a state of terror. Absolute terror! If I'd been going up to receive the devil — instead of God — I couldn't have felt worse. I'm still trying to figure that one out. About this time too, aged seven, I was playing in Hyde Park when suddenly a man in RAF uniform appeared like an apparition, standing there with his prick hanging out. He flashed a silver coin and, pointing to his prick, said 'Come and suck this like a lollipop.' For some reason I can't yet explain, I did. I moved towards him like a clockwork doll. Then, as soon as I began to do as he had asked I began to retch, and very quickly I was being sick — vomiting, vomiting, vomiting. When I looked up again he was gone. Disappearance of RAF man!

After the war Diana was sent to a boarding-school for a short time, but was immediately removed once she had informed her father that she had learned about sex from an older girl. So, having already been twice uprooted, once by the arbitrary rules of war, once by a paternal capriciousness stemming from fear of a daughter's nascent sexual knowledge, Christina returned to Knightsbridge, to a home where the mother was all but invisible and the father dominant. Christina was sent to Kensington's Lycée Française.

We lived above this cafe which my parents owned in Knightsbridge. My father had lived in Switzerland for most of his childhood, and he liked the idea of me learning French. He was also very conscious of money, power and status. Some unpleasant experiences as a child had made him aware of the difference between those who have power and those who haven't and he was specially ambitious for me. In his sociable moods he would tell others of my high-grade academic abilities and of my fearlessness. With pride he would say, 'She'll marry a millionaire.' He had no reason to doubt this since I was associating with millionaires' sons at the Lycée. Besides, he'd made his little fortune unaided and was now living in a classy area of London, even though he'd arrived from a little village in Switzerland. He therefore saw no limits to my possibilities.

My relationship with my father was very ambiguous. I was the apple of his eye and I liked to impress him. Yet, at the same time, at some subterranean level of our relationship I was in terror of him. I sensed him as an ogre-type man who could suddenly go berserk. I pictured him running amok with an axe; it was a constant dread of an ultimate battering. Father had total command and control. Mother was a timid lady who would say black was white to keep the peace with him. She was totally powerless. I felt sorry for her. I only saw my father hit my mother once but I knew she always had it hanging over her head. He had a bull-neck look about him and was powerfully built. The trouble was that you never knew when his mood would change. If, for instance, he could not find a pencil exactly where it should have been, that was it, he would be in a rage in a flash. Over and over again I would catch my mother crying in her bedroom, and when I would beg her to leave him, she would always say, 'He doesn't mean it. He can't help it.' But one day when I pressed her even more than usual, she added, 'What would we do without him?' in a most sad and pathetic tone, and that boggled my mind. It was beyond me, but one thing was for sure: for me the whole situation was unbearable.

Getting Out

Meanwhile, I was at the Lycée and I got on well there with my lessons. It was during this period that I first began to steal regularly. In fact, every day I was stealing a tiny amount from each pocket in the senior-school cloakroom. I would also steal a small amount from my parents' shop till and my mother's handbag. Out on the street I would con people out of money. I never told a soul, it was my deep, dark secret. I'm still trying to work out *why* I did it. Out of school I played with the LCC[2] kids on bombsites, ringing doorbells and running away and doing other silly things like that. We went swimming a lot, but only to play rough games together. I used a lot of the stolen money to buy these chums of mine cheese and tomato rolls, comics, ice-creams and such. They were all boys. Most evenings I was allowed out until nine to nine-thirty. After a hard day's work in the café our parents were only too pleased, as long as our homework was done, for us to go out and play so that they could have peace and quiet.

Eventually, after a discussion with the Head of the Lycée, Diana's father decided that his daughter would benefit from a stricter regime. This was not because of her stealing, for Diana had never been caught — mainly because the money stolen from the rich Lycée pupils had never been missed! Nor was it just because of her wildness, the wildness which had previously made her father so proud. No, the new factor in the situation was the onset of menstruation. With the coming of Diana's periods, her father began sharply to differentiate between the very few degrees of freedom which Diana could have and the much greater latitude to be allowed her brother. The tomboy of childhood had to be somehow groomed into being the sort of woman that a millionaire would want to marry. Diana was sent to a Convent Boarding School in Barnet. When she was soon expelled from there for wandering abroad late at night she returned home to attend London's Brompton Oratory School as a day pupil. It was then that she engaged in the series of expoits which were to bring her into a head-on collision with her father. At this time, too, she was suddenly made aware that not only was she not one of the boys biologically, but that also, socially, she was no longer to be seen as being 'one of them'.

While I was still at the Lycée my periods started and I was late getting to school that day. When I was asked what had delayed me I told them. Jacques, a boy in my class, became tearful and said, 'Poor Diana', just as though he sensed all the troubles which were going to be in store for me now that I'd become a woman. The Lycée boys always did seem to have a protectiveness towards me, though I cannot say why. They were polar opposites to the LCC boys. Once I started my periods the LCC boys just got randy with me and wanted to play 'Truth, dare, kiss or promise' — with me as the one they all wanted to kiss! I didn't like kissing at all. That was the beginning of my troubles. As I experienced it, my mates had turned against me. They suddenly saw me as female. It was the end of my fun. My father's attitude towards me was changing too. Previously he had been proud of my independent spirit and had often said that I should have been a *boy*, meaning it as a compliment of course. Now that I was growing up he did not feel able to explain away my independent spirit by saying that I should have been a *man*! He was out of his depth and he was scared of what might become of me. He decided therefore that what I needed was a rigid discipline. In his more optimistic moments he would still say that I would marry a millionaire, but more and more frequently I now heard the prediction that I would end up in the gutter.

Diana's independent behaviour was an affront to her father's hopes; additionally, he could not tolerate the disobedience of a young teenage daughter. Eventually, therefore, he took Diana to court as being beyond his control and in moral danger. She, as a consequence of his inability to cope with her, was thereafter seen as being in need of state protection. She was placed on probation with a curfew condition. Diana, for her part, felt that she could not be the kind of growing-up daughter that her father wished her to be. Certainly she was growing-up but, paradoxically, the more she became conscious of her burgeoning adulthood, the more her father tried to straight-jacket her into a discipline which he had never actually imposed upon her when she had been a child. Brian, a twenty-four year old man whom she met one day at a swimming pool, had what to Diana at that time was a major attraction — he treated her like an adult. Flattered by his attention and fascinated by his conversation, she spent an evening with him. Then, terrified of her father's likely reaction when she discovered that the hour was even later than she had ever been out alone before, she accepted Brian's offer to sleep at his place for the night. Because he seemed such a well-bred type of man — he was, in fact, a sculptor — Diana never anticipated the possibility of any trouble whatsoever. On the contrary, she considered herself very lucky that such a handsome and interesting man was coming to her rescue by protecting her in her time of need. That night Brian attempted to rape her. Next day, she felt that she was indeed between the devil and the deep blue sea. She did not have to wonder for long which way she should jump. Upon her return home her father packed her off to the police station. Diana was now on the road to Approved School.

I'd really been raped through and through, even though not vaginally, because, after an all-night struggle, just as I had lost all my strength, he rushed towards me to have sex and came — before he got in — on my leg. Next minute he was down on his knees sobbing, 'I'll get seven years for this.' I was in a state of terror and utter confusion. I feared that as I was the only 'witness' he might kill me there and then. I also feared that he might start trying to rape me all over again. Because he now seemed so very pathetic I also felt sorry for him. And because I so dreaded facing my father, I was wishing Brian could just promise me that he would never turn into a beast-of-a-man again, so that I could stay with him. Equally I knew that whatever he said I would never be able to trust him again. He let me go, and for me there seemed nowhere to turn anymore. I jumped on a bus and went home. I rang the bell. Dad came down, opened the door, said 'Go to Gerrard Road Police Station,' and slammed the door. I arrived there in a pitiable state of nervous exhaustion and I was immediately cross-questioned about where I'd been. I wouldn't tell them where for two reasons. First, I wanted to protect Brian from the seven years imprisonment that he had seemed so sure that he'd get. Although I hated what he had done to me, he had been so nice to me the rest of the time that I could not fit him into the stereotype of a man who went to prison at all, let alone for years! He looked like a true-blue hero of the cinema. Because of this, when he turned into a rapist during the night, I saw it as a freak insanity streak in him — a sort of brainstorm — which he needed help with, not punishment. Secondly, the police approach put me off them completely. As soon as I told them I'd slept in Hyde Park for the night, they aggressively threatened me with Approved School if I didn't tell the truth. Then they threatened me with a vaginal examination in order to *prove* the truth. Dictatorial and tyrannical, they reminded me of my father at his worst.

By now I was feeling very woebegone indeed, but I stuck to my story. (As time went on I was to learn that it was never the screws and the cops who were my worst enemies; it was always the 'thugs' in my bedroom!) Next thing I knew I'd got to be examined. As I was so exhausted I was soon overcome when I tried to resist having to lie down and have my legs pulled open. I heard them say 'virgo intacta' — and that there was bruising. I can well remember being conscious of the irony of being seen as 'virgo intacta'! At that moment I knew that though a rose by any other name might smell as sweetly, bullshit by any other name could smell as lousily.

After another court appearance it was decided that as Diana was beyond her parents' control, in 'moral danger' and in breach of probation, she should be sent to an Approved School.

Tina — Teenage Prostitute

At Approved School Diana (now Tina) learned some new lessons.

When the lights went off in the dorm that first night, all the women were suddenly scurrying all over the place. Lots were diving into each other's beds. It was lesbianism rampant. For some reason unknown to me I had the idea that lesbianism (I first heard the word in there) was even worse than hetero-sexuality. Next day, a woman who, I'd heard, was lesbian, came over to the table to speak to me. I said something to the effect that I didn't want to speak to her as she was a 'fucking lesbian' (it was impossible not to swear in there without being seen as a cissy and be bullied accordingly) and then she went for me. I retaliated and a fight developed. Fights in there were always stopped anyway before they could become really dangerous. As it turned out it was the best thing that could have happened for me, because she was the leader of the 'heavy mob' in there. I, sublimely ignorant of her reputation anyway, fearlessly and effectively gave at least as good as I got. My reputation was made. I learned the ropes very quickly after that.

Next came Bette.

I fell head over heels in love. She was four years older than me and she was a 'recall', meaning that she'd been there before and, though she had not committed a crime, had breached her licence. She knew the score through and through. Looking back, I see that it was hero-worship on my part. All I know is that at the time she was the be-all and end-all to me. The only thing was that I was still such a sexless being. I didn't want sex and she did — being accustomed to lesbianism. I'm not sure whether it was Bette who actually 'took my virginity' or not — it could have been. The way I saw it I had been 'raped' by Brian and what really happened after that, had, as far as I was concerned, no bearing on my virginal state.

When Tina and Bette absconded to London together, they attempted at first to get regular work in the Employment Centre until they realized that they could not do so without enquiries being made which would reveal that Tina should still have been at school. Because Tina, unlike Bette, had the conventional good looks which men are usually expected to go for, Bette suggested that Tina earn money by prostituting.

She told me to stand on the corner of Curzon Street and to say 'Five pounds, short-time' when approached. I smile now when I recall that she quite forgot to tell me how short a short-time was! The first man came up in a fancy car. Bowler hat. English gentleman. 'Hello', I said 'Five pounds, short-time.' 'Jump in,' he said, 'where do we go?' That threw me. Where does one go? He said, 'It's alright, I've got somewhere we can go to.' Relief, relief! His town flat — beautiful place, back of Curzon Street, back of Park Lane. In we went. There was a big settee and I sat right in the middle, perched on the edge with my knees together, trying to look as sophisticatedly grown-up as possible. I was *very* worried lest he suspect my age and call the police. He took his coat off and said, 'Don't you think we should go into the bedroom?' 'Yes, of course,' I said, and went and sat on the bed in exactly the same position as before, watching him undress. Then he said 'Don't you think you should take your knickers off?' I was hastily beginning to take them off, when he shot across the room, intending to have sex with me straight away. Instead, he came — on my leg! Of course, I can see now what I couldn't see then — I'd got Approved School knickers on and I looked very young. Some men would get their kicks from just that. My instant feeling was one of disgust at the mess on my legs, and I wanted to get away from the whole sorry business. Having washed the mess away, I was just about to leave through the front door of the flat when he said, 'Just a minute, how long have you been doing this?' Panic, panic, keep calm! Coolly I replied, 'Four years, why?' 'Well, didn't anyone ever tell you to ask for the money first?' What a boob I'd made! I've no notion how the money could have gone out of my head. Quick as a flash I said, 'I do always ask for the money first but I knew that in your case I didn't have to — that I could trust you.' First he handed me the one five pound note, then he pulled out another one, saying, 'And this one's for luck'. That changed everything. At that rate, I didn't mind getting a mess on my leg.

Bette and Tina were soon caught and Bette was sent to Borstal. Meanwhile Tina's life became a constant round of running away from Approved School, being caught and absconding again. And there were always the men who were ready to aid and abet in return for sex.

Once when I ran away I was arrested and charged with indecency, for wanking a man in the back of a car. It was in a dark alley at night and the police could only see us because they were shining torches into cars and peering in. Because it was a prostitute area I was charged. The man concerned was lucky not to be charged with having sex with a minor, especially since, as it turned out, he was a married man. Other times I used to give myself up because the world of sex

and men made me feel so miserable. But back in Approved
School I'd soon shin down yet another four-storey drainpipe
and run away again. I couldn't just give up on the world.
After I'd run from the Approved School I'd get a lift on a
lorry. All the lorry drivers, with one exception, wanted sex,
and I was often put out in the middle of nowhere because I
refused. Sometimes I felt it was better to get it over with,
other times I'd be stubborn. No morals, just my mood.

In winter time Tina would first break into a house to get a coat to
hide her school-uniform dress. Then she would set out to look for
someone who would give her the friendship and security which she
needed.

I was always hoping to meet a man who would be different to
the rest. At that age, and in those days, I had no notion of
stereotypical social behaviour. I didn't know that every man
who made a friendly approach towards me would secretly be
expecting sex, and that as soon as I accepted the offer of a
meal or a drink, he'd be thinking his chances were good. I
didn't know that in fact such offers were sexual traps. I didn't
know that men were supposed to con women into believing
that they were not after sex, whilst women were always
expected to say 'no' when they really meant 'yes'. On the face
of it, how was one to know of such stupidities! The result was
that I could never get used to the fact that, regardless of
whether they were well-educated businessmen, ordinary
working men, artists, athletes, academics — even a priest one
time — they all wanted sex. Further, they didn't seem to care
that they had a totally unresponsive female who was actually
like a zombie — I was later to call myself a rubber dolly.

It usually happened like this: being alone and having
nowhere to live, I would, when approached, agree to go for
an evening meal or a drink. During subsequent conversation
I would let it be known that I disliked sex and had nowhere to
live. Generally the reaction was an offer of a bed and a
promise that there would be no sex. Later, once we got into
bed, it was as if I was with a different man and I would be
pressurised for sex. At that hour of the night my alternatives
would be even less viable than usual. It would seem to me

that I had little choice but to stay and get it over with as quickly as possible. I soon discovered, however, that although he (whoever he was) could then invariably get straight off to sleep, I, in my silent rage, could not. So, as soon as I was sure that he was sufficiently fast asleep, I would whisper 'John, John', (or 'Dick' or 'Harry'). When I got no reply I would stealthily creep out of the bed, look round for a bottle ready to attack him with if he awoke, rob him, and leave him. I'd then run out into the night to a bed-and-breakfast place to sleep.

Once, though, I had closed the door quietly behind me when I discovered that I still had an orange-juice bottle in my hand. I put it down beside the door but I bumped into the man later in the Edgware Road. He said, 'Look, I don't really mind about the money [forty-four pounds], but what was the orange-juice bottle doing outside my door?' and although I could have told him a lie, I chose to tell him that it was to hit him over the head with if he had woken up. I can't remember what he said. We didn't carry on the conversation after that. He just disappeared!

So, ironically, this was life for the young teenager who had been sent away from home as being beyond control and in moral danger. But, wherever she was, Tina could not make sense of a society which concomitantly recognized, exploited and then denied to her her sexuality. At the same time, since she could not get a job whilst she was on the run — and would anyway have been unlikely to get a job that paid her enough to set up in a place of her own — Tina had little alternative but to remain hopeful that one day she would meet a decent man, even though her experiences were teaching her that she could expect to be betrayed over and over again.

To me, then, every man was a potential saviour. Looking back now I can see that, as I walked down the road, my desperate needs must have been apparent to every man who fancied his chances. I was at a complete loose end and I was not sophisticated enough to know how to hide the signs. That's the reason I was also getting re-arrested so frequently! Despite the reality of my life's experiences, I was being driven by my need to find love. Also, at that so tender age, I was too impressed by the power of the adult world to imagine that I could be anything but a winner when I became a proper adult myself.

Chris — Borstal Girl

Now I was fifteen. Instead of being taken back to Approved School when I was recaptured, I was taken to Holloway Prison and diagnosed as a persistent absconder. This was actually my second time in Holloway. The last time I had spent the whole two weeks in punishment because I had put up a struggle when they took my cigarettes away from me. This time, I was to be straight-jacketed, injected and placed into the 'dungeons' of the place as soon as I reacted angrily over being the only remand prisoner not allowed to smoke — because I was too young!

Anyway, that's all by the by. Here I was in Holloway for the second time. I had to stay there until my sixteenth birthday when I would be old enough to go to Borstal. In retrospect it seems rather silly that they didn't just let me go free at this stage, since the only reason I was in all this trouble was that I was in 'moral danger', since I had in any case already had an enormous dose of that 'moral danger' and since I was now sixteen, and legally entitled to have sex. But they didn't. Instead, I was now defined as a persistent absconder — the authorities could not control me either! Many years later my father was to tell me that he'd never have asked them to control me if he'd have known I could run away. And I must say that I can see his point, even though his words did remind me of the Monopoly game: go straight to prison, don't stop at 'go' and don't collect £200 along the way! For being a persistent absconder, I was sent to Borstal Training. I was to stay there twenty-two months. At the end of that time I was defined as being 'untrainable'.

The prospect of Borstal held no terrors for Tina. Quite the opposite, in fact. For Tina thought that in the Borstal wing of Aylesbury prison she would be reunited with the only person who had ever really mattered to her since she had left home — her beloved Bette. Desolation followed. Bette, on a different wing of the prison and in love with another girl, wanted nothing to do with Tina for fear of making the other girl jealous.

My whole world then went to pieces. I smashed the contents of my cell, smashed the glass in the tiny windows, and cut my wrist. Then because, instead of allowing me to cool down first, they attempted to drag me off to punishment, I smashed a screw over the shoulder with the leg of the wash-stand. Bang, smash, wallop, straight into punishment on my first day in Borstal! I spent months in isolation. I would have got out much quicker but I refused to sew the mailbags which were a part of the punishment. The truth was that I needed the privacy in which to nurse away my heartache and I would not come out until I felt sufficiently hardened against it.

When I finally did come out, what a reputation I had! I got stacks of love-letters. I was king of the castle. This is when I changed from Tina to Chris. I suddenly became the love 'em and leave 'em woman and changed from Tina to Chris. I was in my element, playing the macho. Borstal suited me well in this respect because nobody ever touched me sexually. I learned that being macho (butch) was a way of having sexual power — and in that connection, and carried away by that image of myself, I did one thing at that time that I now feel very ashamed of. There was one woman there, very quiet, a stubborn sort of woman who kept herself to herself and seemed to me too unimpressed by my status in there. One day I made an attack on her with a few other women. You could almost call it a gang-bang rape, but it wasn't, because no one touched her but me. I know that I only used my fingers, but if she had been a virgin she wouldn't have been after that . . . I then never gave her another thought, until many years later.

Chris — Ponce, Prostitute and Robber

I was coming up to eighteen when they let me out of Borstal. I went home to mum and dad and got a job as a petrol-pump attendant. My father had decided to give me another chance, but, unfortunately it turned out that there was no way that it could possibly work between us. Even though he knew of my experiences and even though I was now earning my own living, I was flabbergasted to discover that he still had the same proprietary attitude towards me. The first time that I got ready to go to a dance at the Astoria dance-hall, my father stopped me and would not allow me to go because I had no escort whom he approved of! That night I left home and by so doing breached my Borstal licence.

I went and joined a group of people at a drinking-club in the West End, a club I'd heard about when I was in Borstal. It was mostly frequented by thieves and prostitutes. This was when I suddenly decided to dress as a man. In those days there was no unisex way of dressing. It was definitely either a man's way or a woman's way and my men's clothes were so effective that sometimes I would be called 'Sir' in shops. I remember thinking that this was a clever way of ensuring that I wouldn't be chatted up any more — a way of getting out of the sex arena. I went on to be a ponce (or pimp). For a while I was with two women at the same time. One woman was the 'goody' and I was her butch lover, the other woman was a prostitute. I would get the money earned by the prostitute and use it to squire the 'goody' around town. With the prostitute I behaved in a bullying and arrogant macho fashion, while she acted out the role of the submissive little-woman. However within weeks I was arrested again. This time I was sent to Exeter Prison and spent eight months there for being in breach of my licence. Later I came to see poncing as not being a very nice thing to do — but by then I'd become a burglar!

Chris spent more time in prison. In and out she went, her life inside prison becoming an extension of her life outside — and vice versa.

I know it seems as though I was out and about a lot, but, in fact, from the age of fourteen to twenty I only had six month's freedom altogether. Whenever I got loose I behaved like children do when let loose from the disciplined constraints of the classroom — I rushed out into the playground and packed in one hell of a lot of playing. Once I was only out eleven days and I had twenty-one charges of stealing from cars taken into consideration! Mind you, sometimes I would admit to charges I hadn't done, just to show-off.

I didn't question the rights and wrongs of it all. No more than, I assume, men question the rights and wrongs of conning women in order to use them sexually. I just did what felt right to me. It was far easier to focus on the rights and wrongs of other people, and the world in general, but even that was done in a diffused sort of way. Everybody seemed to mouth righteousness and practise its opposite, one way or another. Besides, in a world where tens of thousands of children were legitimately murdered during wartime what could anyone say? Since some of the best brains in the land, those who rule the rest, are incapable of putting a stop to mass slaughter once and for all . . . well we all do our best I suppose, and maybe we were all just doing what came naturally. I know that I was, even though none of it made any sense to me. About this time, a probation officer summed me up in a report for a court case. She said that I was of superior intelligence, unamenable to reason, indifferent to suggestion and altogether a law unto myself. Furthermore, that all my associates were prostitutes and thieves. That said it all, and I felt highly flattered. Which brings to mind *Alice in Wonderland*!

After serving an eighteen months' sentence for shopbreaking, I came out aged twenty. I then met some women I knew from the past who had a one-room set-up which was designed for 'robbing the "steamers" ', the name which we gave to men who used prostitutes. There was one bed in this room and what seemed like a makeshift wardrobe behind slightly-open curtains. Just in front of the curtain-rail there was an armchair. The light was a dim red one. The men had a choice of putting their clothes on the floor, the bed or the armchair and they nearly always chose the chair. Whenever possible we had music on the radio, turned low. There were five of us using the room. Someone would be hidden behind the chair, ready to rob from the men's clothes. We used hand signals to communicate while the man was on the bed having sex and we made sure to keep his face turned away. One hand signal would mean, 'Lots of money; keep talking; walk out of the block with him; make sure he doesn't pay much notice to where he is.' Another meant, 'Get rid of him quickly, nothing worth robbing.' For a short while I was in my element because I was getting my own back on men. Then I experienced it as being bad for me and suddenly turned against it. Shortly after, I stopped prostituting altogether.

Two months after coming out of Holloway prison Chris got married and immediately became pregnant.

I had to contact my father for his consent to my marriage because in law I was still a minor. The first thing that he said to my prospective husband was, 'Do you know all about her?'. He replied 'Yes'. My father found the proposition appealing because he thought that marriage would make me respectable. My husband assumed that I would change once I was married. I vaguely imagined that marriage in itself would automatically effect a change in me. There was also another factor; I had already decided that I wanted a little girl. It was as if I could start all over again with her and put her wise to authority and men. With his looks and my wits, I reasoned, we could have a lovely little girl, the corrected version of me. So when I had a son instead of a daughter it threw me for a while. My husband also had completely unrealistic expectations of me as a wife and housekeeper. Looking back I can see that each of us, in our own ways, was conditioned to a specific view of the wife role. He was aggressively demanding that I live up to his view. I, resentful both of his tyrannical attitude and his male freedom from any such role expectations, kept running away from him.

At the same time I was also secretly feeling guilty, not only for not living up to his expectations, but also for not even *wanting* to live up to them. For, by overtly defying the marital stereotype — sexually, domestically and financially — I was trying to assert my right to be treated in a friendly and respectful way as the individual I actually was. On a deeper level I felt terrified that in so doing I might, in fact, be hyper-arrogantly defying the natural laws of creation. And if that were so then I was nothing more than a wicked freak!

Needless to say, I kept this feeling as suppressed as I was able, but whilst I was enmeshed in these seemingly irreconcileable conflicts my pattern of life, not surprisingly, became one of running away from my husband, being found by him, returning to him and, in no time, running away again. I never lived with him for longer than two weeks at a time.

I did finally manage to stay away from him for quite a while once I had found a place which made me willing to leave London. I took the baby with me and moved in with an ex-girlfriend in Hove. Suddenly a ton weight seemed to be lifted from my shoulders. In Valerie I had a ready-made nanny and housekeeper and there was no sex. Valerie enjoyed domesticity, I enjoyed being the provider. I had learnt that you could get hold of skeleton keys that would open any mortice lock. Once I had acquired these keys and got the necessary celluloid for opening the Yale locks too, I was set up to be a professional burglar all on my own. In the evenings I would often go to some of the clubs in Brighton and enjoy men's company. I soon became friendly with a group of thieves there, but I totally avoided all sexual encounters. I was making hundreds of pounds a week. I was enjoying my son. It was to prove to be one of the very best times of my life. It lasted three months.

Her husband sought her out and Chris, conceding that the baby needed a father, returned with him to London. During the first two years of her marriage she kept out of gaol and then, when she was pregnant with her second child, a daughter, the round of court appearances, remands and gaol sentences started again — with the added complications of children, pregnancies and abortions.

I did a couple of two-year prison sentences during my marriage. One was for burglary, the other for a conspiracy charge appertaining to sixteen months of various forms of theft. I was released from my last prison sentence, served when I was already divorced, at the age of thirty-one; and from the day I got married at twenty, to the beginning of that last sentence when I was twenty-nine, I had had six years out of prison. During that six years, as well as having the two children, I had three abortions and one miscarriage. I had someone do the first two abortions, the last one I did myself. All the women I knew were doing it, and so were all the women they knew! Looking back it amazes me where we got the courage from since we'd all heard of women who had died whilst having these illegal abortions. They'd die because of shock to the system or an air bubble in the blood stream. I'd even met women in prison serving long sentences for having committed fatal abortions. In those days it was almost impossible to get a legal abortion, unless you were rich, of course, and had the right connections. Although I could have afforded the rich person's fee, I didn't even try to find the necessary connection since that belonged to the conventional world. What I mean is, it wasn't the underworld's way of going about breaking the law and my world was the underworld.

Chris — Mother and Shoplifter

Each time Chris came out of prison her first priority was to get a place so that she could get her children out of care. By 1963 she was no longer living with her husband and was determined to do her best as a single parent. After a two-year sentence completed in 1963 she came out of prison and met a group of people who were quite heavily| into hashish smoking. Chris was soon to come to appreciate the cathartic effect that hashish could have upon her frenetic existence. To date she had never really fancied shoplifting. Within a short time, however, she had formed a shoplifting gang.

This is how it all began. I was in a shop in Oxford Street one busy Saturday and I was in a terrible hurry. I was buying three dresses for my daughter and I couldn't get an assistant. That was when I though of the expediency of stealing the dresses. In the end I paid for two and stole one. The following Monday I went into a big store in Oxford Street and stole a whole load of other things. Shortly afterwards I met a woman who was willing to come and shoplift with me — a woman whom I considered to be an advantage to have with me. All that we now needed was a driver. We soon found one. The driver mixed with a group of people who smoked marihuana, or hashish, every day and that was when I started Smoking.[3] I had tried it out previously a couple of times but had remained unimpressed. Now, however, I was to find that it really suited me.

Like many other money-earning mothers, particularly those who are single parents, Chris now attempted to become Superwoman — good mother, good earner, good playmate.

I'd get my children ready for school in the morning, go to work, collect the children after school, take them home, cook them supper, entertain them, bathe them, put them to bed — and, Bob's your uncle, it was my turn to go and have fun. I was earning very good money again and the Smoke calmed my nerves and helped me to be a much more relaxed mother. Shoplifting pumps up the adrenalin, puts you on edge. It's like a lucky dip situation with a difference: put your hand in, take this, take that. But if you're not careful, suddenly a hand on your arm, and you're in gaol. I must say that it does seem strange to me now how I never saw the enormous incompatability in the situation of being a full-time mother and a full-time thief. The two areas were, at this time, still in completely different compartments of myself. Being a thief felt even more natural to me than being a mother did; as a provider I could claim the same privilege as any father who chooses a risky way of earning a living. So, after I'd fetched the children from school I would send them into the garden or into their room saying, 'Mummy's going to have a rest for ten minutes in her room.' I'd have a Smoke (the way conventional mums have Valium) and be completely relaxed to rejoin the children. I always went to work sober though. By work I mean shoplifting; I thought of it as my worktime, and I treated it accordingly.

Chris felt competent. Even the prospect of a gaol sentence did not intimidate her. As a professional criminal Chris could look upon gaol as an occupational hazard; not one to be sought after, of course, but one, nonetheless, to be viewed with stoicism. And if the worst came to the worst, she knew that she could carry off a prison sentence with style and aplomb.

As it happened, one of the local policemen very much fancied the woman I was working with. One day he told her that the Flying Squad were coming to the area to watch my flat. Naturally, she told me and the driver. We then all decided to stop going to the shops for a while. We went drinking instead of working, but we were very bored and very much missed the shoplifting. After only four days we all agreed that it would be O.K. to get back to work. We didn't even look out for the spying police in the van parked opposite my flat. Soon after that we all arrived back at my place with the car loaded — and the police just pounced from everywhere. The three of us were arrested and landed in the Old Bailey on the conspiracy charge I've already mentioned. The charge went back sixteen months and included stealing, receiving — a load of charges. The trial lasted fourteen days and we got two years each. As long as I knew the children were OK then I was OK. (Throughout the whole of my prison career there was only one occasion when I heard that there was a problem and, luckily for me and the children, the prison social worker, whom I contacted, was both able and willing to quickly remedy the situation.) As for myself, the arrest had been adventurous and the court case too. We mostly laughed our way through the prison sentence. That's how we were.

Chris — Gaolbird

The year was 1964 and Chris was at the height of her criminal career. Unbeknown to her, however, the time was fast approaching when the laughing would be over, though it was to be 1966 before her criminal career would begin to go downhill all the way. From the early sixties Chris's life had been hectic. She had not only been a fun-loving career woman, she had also been mothering her two children and acting as their sole provider. During the same period she had undergone a series of pregnancies and abortions, had a miscarriage and experienced stressful and often violent relationships with men. On every front she had been winding herself up mentally, emotionally and physically to an extreme of exertion that was later to tell on even her strong physique. But this was to be in the future. In 1964 the only immediate brake upon the fun was her meeting with a prison psychiatrist. Because he was not morally judgmental of her behaviour and she did not perceive him as being flirtatious, Chris was prepared to give him a hearing. This, unremarked by her at the time, was the beginning of the end of her criminal life as she had previously perceived it.

> On the 1964 sentence I met a psychiatrist. He wasn't the first I'd met in gaol but this one, unlike the others, was to make a great impression on me. He had a very non-critical view of me. The first time that I met him I sat there telling him how capable I was, how *little* I needed a psychiatrist, in fact. In order to impress him with just how little I needed help I told him that I could get cannabis whenever I wanted it. Of course, I see now that the very things which I was telling him to demonstrate my capability were the very things which, in the eyes of the world, would have proved that I was incapable! At the end of the interview, just as I was about to leave, he asked me: 'Why do you keep coming back to prison?'. 'I keep getting caught,' I replied. 'Why do you keep getting caught?' he asked. 'Because I'm unlucky.' Then I added, 'Most times it's "through information received".' He said, 'that's not the reason you keep coming back to prison.' *I stopped dead and looked at him.* He said, 'You wouldn't come back to prison if you didn't want to.' I left the office and went quickly to the group of women who were waiting to see him and said, 'I've really got to warn you: this psychiatrist is completely mad.'

Soon after Chris's first encounter with the psychiatrist, a selected group of women were allowed out of their cells, two evenings a week, for discussions with him.

> All we had to do was to chat amongst ourselves. His words had made an impression on me. I began to examine the ways in which I had been caught. I didn't have to look far. This last time we had been told on good authority that the police were watching us, yet we had left it for only four days before starting again! Why had we done that? We were intelligent women and yet we had behaved like idiots.

The psychiatrist kept in touch with Chris after she had finished her sentence. She visited his consulting rooms in Harley Street and later joined a therapeutic discussion group which he was running. She was flattered that an intelligent male could be so attracted by her mind rather than her body. He confirmed what she had always known; that she was more, much more, than a sex object and further, that she was certainly not a sex object gone wrong. Additionally, he also made good sense of dimensions of her character which had puzzled her.

He was the first person to confirm a side of me which no-one else had been able to accept. He said, 'Although you allow men to have sex with you, you don't want them to.' He said it as though not wanting to have sex could be seen as quite OK. Because of this acceptance I found myself able to question this area of my life less defensively. Then I discovered, to my dismay, that I had actually been behaving in a way that could easily be interpreted as being flirtatious towards men. Unable to make sense of it, I finally asked Dr. P. 'Why do I flirt with men, then?' His answer was, 'You want them to admire you.' As soon as he said it I knew that he was right.

But time was to prove that Chris had been independent of others' definitions for too long to take without question even the advice of someone whom she so admired. She still chose to provide for herself and her children and she still chose to practise her skills at shoplifting — an occupation which provided her with the twin necessities of kicks and high income.

One day Dr. P. said to me, 'I think you should come into the hostel [a place which catered for female ex-prisoners who were having difficulties in coping] or you will be getting arrested again very soon.' I said, 'Don't be silly, I can't do that, I've got my children to look after. I'm just tired, so I'm going off to the South of France for a holiday.' He said, 'You'll go for a holiday and when you come back it will be exactly the same.' I shut my ears to what he was telling me. Off I went on holiday, taking my son aged nine, my daughter aged seven, and my brother's little girl aged eight with me. It was 1966. I came back and a few days later I was arrested in a big London hotel and was charged with shoplifting jewellery. I claimed 'No case to answer', and was found not guilty. While I had been on bail, however, I had been arrested again. I had joined up with a group of people whom I scarcely knew. I knew that this was a dangerous thing to do but I was closing my ears to my own common sense as well as to Dr. P's. At that time, I was living beyond my strength, but I did not realize this — I thought I was someone who was powerfully strong and on top of things. Then one day I went to pieces.

I had just agreed to give someone some money. I often helped people who were in financial need as part of my strong, capable, image. So there I was, feeling powerful, when a bluebottle streaked across the room towards the middle of my forehead, then ducked away. The next minute I had crumpled in my seat. When I put my daughter to bed that night, in shadow she looked like my mother come to haunt me from the dead. I had become phobic. I was alright until it was the children's bedtime then, alone in a silent flat, I'd get into a frenzied state of fear. The only solution was to swiftly smoke a joint and rush off to join the people I associated with in the clubs, taking three or four joints with me and smoking them in secret in the toilet because these people, all being boozers, looked down on drug-takers. From then on I lost my professionalism as a thief. My nerves were shattered and it showed. I should have had the sense to stop thieving altogether and go into that hostel after all, but my reasoning powers were, by now, quite overruled by my internal emotional conflicts. Soon I was arrested again, for ten-thousand pounds' worth of jewellery. When I had been arrested for the hotel robbery, Dr. P. had said, 'I warned you that this would happen.' I replied, 'Ah, yes, but I was wrongfully arrested, and I expect to be found "not guilty".' 'In that case', he said, 'next time you're arrested you'll make sure you're found guilty.' He was absolutely right. When the police had arrived at my flat I had known that they were coming because one of the members of the group had already been arrested for the same offence and, by then, we had already all known that a member of the group was the informer. I could easily have got rid of the hashish which was in one of my handbags. But I hadn't. So when the police came they found it and I panicked, fearing that they might see me as a drug-taker who was unfit to be a mother. Now I can see that it was all nonsense, but then I promptly made a deal with them. 'If you throw away that hashish and pretend that you haven't seen it I will admit to the jewellery.' They, of course, were delighted and couldn't believe it. Not until I was actually signing the statement did Dr. P.'s words come back to me.

From then on Chris had to live with the tensions engendered by the struggle between criminality and motherhood. She had realized that there was a possibility of a five to seven-year sentence, but she was surprised when she later learnt that the two barristers involved in the case had betted on twelve to fourteen years. In fact, as a result of the sympathetic report of Dr. P. and its favourable reception by the judge, Chris received only a two-year sentence. But there was little time to triumph. The ties of motherhood, which Chris had for so long both embraced and rejected, were now making themselves felt in a way that she could never have anticipated.

I was not the same woman going into prison this time. I'd no sooner arrived there and was up on the fourth landing when suddenly I heard my son calling me, 'Mummy, Mummy'. Part of me knew that it was not possible but I kept on hearing him. I rushed to the tiny ledge and climbed up on it so that I could try to get a view of the yard down below. I banged on the door feeling demented with grief. The screws came running. 'What are you talking about? You know your son's not here. This is not like you, pull yourself together,' they said. I replied 'I know he can't be here, but he must be needing me — it's telepathy!' Then I added, 'Please let me ring him, at least.' They said, 'No, you know we can't let you do that.' In no time at all I began a round of smashing, crashing and fighting the other women. I was put in punishment over and over again. Then it happened. During a period in punishment in solitary confinement, I forgave my mother. Indeed I felt that I had no cause to forgive her really, since at that time I was seeing myself as being worse than her as a mother. Magic happened to me then. I felt as though all tensions were melting away in the base of my skull and, in a flash, I was

completely transformed. I rose up renewed both physically
and emotionally. I had a feeling of complete harmony and
bliss with the whole of creation. Everyone looked like tall,
beautiful children. Sixteen months later everyone was to look
like the devil incarnate. But it did take me sixteen months to
come down. To this day I am still trying to fathom why I had
that experience and what it all meant. Amazingly, during that
time I was also able to heal people's pains by touching them
with my fingers!

At the beginning of that sentence Chris had begun to paint.

Another new and totally unforeseen development in my life
was that I suddenly felt moved to paint. Just before I had
gone into prison someone had shown me a book of paintings
by Bosch and his demonic figures had fascinated me. So soon
after I arrived in prison, when I was allowed to go to the
library, I took out a couple of books of paintings. Whilst
looking through all these paintings I felt, for some reason,
strongly moved to copy three of them. The first was a nun's
face, pure and innocent-looking. The second was that of a
very wild-looking man. The third was of a very artistic-
looking woman. I showed them to Dr. P. and he looked at the
first two saying, 'That's you and that's you — you must get
the two together.' (I then recalled that, funnily enough, the
man I was with before going into prison used to call me a
mixture of Shirley Temple and Humphrey Bogart!) Then the
other women in the prison started pestering me to paint
pictures to put on the walls for Christmas. I told them, 'I can't
paint; it took me ages to copy these three painstakingly —
I've never painted before and I'm not likely to feel like
painting again.' But they kept insisting. So I thought, 'I'll show
them I can't paint; I'll just do any old thing.' I did one after
the other somewhat compulsively; the kind of thing you see
on totem poles — masks. People took them and put them on
the walls. Even though they weren't Christmassy things, they
were colourful.
    Although one was not usually allowed to pursue one's
hobbies whilst in punishment an exception was made in my
case and I was allowed to paint. I started, then, to do really

strange pictures; for instance, one of a very large head filled with snakes, crucifixes, tombstones etc. and a very tiny female body. The Chief Medical Officer in Holloway prison came to see me one day when all these paintings were on the floor. He took one look at them and said, 'They're schizophrenic paintings,' and then added just as he was about to leave, 'Damn bad luck being a psychopath.' Gradually what he had said sunk in. And *he* was the one who decided whether one were sane or not — at this rate I could be sent to Broadmoor! I felt trapped and petrified at the thought. I swiftly became determined that I would not be sent to Broadmoor for nothing. If I were going to be punished as a madwoman then I would behave like one. So I crouched down in the corner by the door, ready to strangle the first person to come in and whilst still in that position I asked myself why, oh why, had Dr. P. not told me that I was insane?

Then suddenly I realized I was *just acting* like a madwoman and I saw myself doing so too. This brought me to my senses immediately. I got up and began to think things out logically. Dr. P. had let me know that there was an extreme split in me, but he'd also given me to understand that it could be resolved. Since I had been his patient for so many years, and he was a consultant psychiatrist, the Chief Medical Officer's power over me was not as total as it was over most of the other women in there. I reasoned therefore that I could trust Dr. P. to know how to handle the situation and I ceased to worry about it. I must say it did occur to me to wonder how on earth I was ever going to get the split in me resolved, but I decided that since I now knew that there was a need to, I *would somehow* find the way, thank goodness. With that thought, and feeling exceedingly exhausted, I lay down and fell asleep.

It was to be much harder than Chris had ever imagined. For *who* was the third party who would get the 'other two' together? *Who* would pay the price for the merger? Whence the capital, whither the product? Time spent in solitary confinement had made her unfit even for the social demands of Askham Grange, an open prison to which she had been sent to finish her sentence. When everything became too difficult for Chris to cope with life at Askham she demanded to be returned to Holloway. She had felt safe in an isolation cell, it represented the one place where no one could demand anything further of her and she could live inside her own dreams. Her life had come to the ironic pass where solitary confinement in a prison-cell represented the only freedom — from the competing demands of earning a living, motherhood and men — which she had experienced since those halcyon pre-puberty days when she had enjoyed the carefree life of tomboy. The transfer to Holloway was refused.

They said, 'You can go into a cell here, if that's all you want.' Hearing it spelt out like that, I began to feel silly. Nevertheless, I went into the cell and curled up as usual into a little ball by the door, round the corner from the spy-hole. Within seconds I was inside my own dreams and soon I was singing, just as I had always done in solitary. But there was a difference; I began to question the sense of it all. So I got up and started to walk up and down, trying to fathom what the hell was going on. Then there was another most unexpected occurrence. The Governor and the Chief Officer came and knocked on the door. They were carrying a dainty tea-tray and they asked if they could have tea with me. The Governor said to me, 'I've known you since you were a young girl and I've always thought of you as being a very intelligent woman. What I don't understand is why you like being in a cell so much.' When I told her that I had just been asking myself the same question for the very first time, she remarked, as she sat there sipping tea, 'Privacy's all very nice, but just how much privacy does anyone need?!' By then I had had enough of the situation. I said, 'Never mind about all that, just get me out of this cell and I won't be coming back.' The Governor immediately complied with my request and I was released from prison soon after that.

It proved to be my last sentence. Having spent a total of nine and a half years in gaol, I was never to be sentenced to a term of imprisonment again. Just before I left Askham Grange I said to the Chief Officer, 'I don't know myself anymore. I haven't a clue what I am going to do when I get out.' 'Take it easy,' she said. 'You'll eventually find your way.' When the taxi driver, who came to take me to the station, said, 'So

you're going home, then' I replied, 'I haven't got a home.'
Then, upon reflection, I added, 'Yes, I have — the world's
my home.'

Christina — A place of her own

During that last sentence I had undergone such exceedingly
traumatic emotional upheavals and such powerfully enlighten-
ing mystical experiences, that by the time I was released I felt
like a cross between someone who had been battered
senseless and someone who had been endowed with a
privileged sort of wisdom. Yet, despite the mystical
experiences, I still had no beliefs. I had seen my mother
praying all her life to no avail. Previously I had lived as if
there were no world other than my own — no politics, no
business. I had never thought about how I could fit into the
conventional world, but, during the next few years, I was to
have to think very seriously about it. Unfortunately so much
of what I was to see in that conventional world appeared to
provide me with retrospective justifications for my earlier
rejections. It mattered to me strongly that I found a
comfortable place in the world. When I had been in prison
there had been a very visible lid and I had imagined that
when it came to the world outside the sky would be the lid —
the limit! But there was just as powerful a lid out here, even
though it was invisible. In fact, it's less like a lid and more like
a giant octopus with many arms. Time and time again it has
seemed to me that, whenever I've managed to make a step
forward, an arm springs out to drag me back. And, although
it's usually got a smiling face, it's got an all-powerful grip.

Christina had decided that the two major sources of her troubles
were to be found in the lawbreaking which was repeatedly landing
her in gaol, and in her relationships with men. At the time of her
release from Askham Grange she had already made three
decisions: to keep out of gaol, to give up crime, and to discover
new and satisfying ways of relating to men. Prior to her last
sentence, all her relationships with men had been very stressful
and Christina had decided that she must discover a way to work

through the emotional barriers which always seemed to arise
between herself and any man with whom she became involved.
She did not think that it would be easy to so completely change her
life, but she did think that with perseverance, hard work, her not
inconsiderable intelligence and the continued development of the
insight gained during her last sentence, she would eventually come
through. It was lucky for her that in April 1968 she could not
possibly have foreseen just how difficult the next sixteen years
were to be. For in addition to turning away from crime, keeping
out of gaol, and improving her relationships with men, she was
equally determined that she would not abandon her obligations as
a mother and that she would strive to realize her own creative and
intellectual potential in a legitimate occupation. (Later she was to
realize that at this stage she had merely tried to swap the bonds of
criminal super-woman for those of conventional super-woman.)
The immediate task, though, was to find somewhere to live.

I saw a notice for a flat-share with a teacher in Brixton and I
moved in. Even the fact that I was living with a teacher was
something quite different for me. True, I had very little to do
with her, as I mostly kept to my own room, but, for the first
time, I was dealing with conventional people, ordinary people,
that up to now I would have drastically avoided.

Next Christina tried to develop a new perspective on men.

When I had been in prison the last time, I had realized that I
might have spent all those years in prison because of weakness
and that it wasn't necessarily something to brag about. I must
say that this was quite a revelation and I began to question
why I had continuously returned to prison. After a great deal
of looking back into my past I realized that spending those
years in prison had been beneficial to me in one important
way: it had, I was convinced, saved me from being murdered!
I had had so many violent encounters with men, and some
very near misses. I had once stabbed a man in self-defence. I
myself had been stabbed because of an unwarranted suspicion
on a man's part. I had twice carried a loaded gun; once to
protect myself from a man who'd already nearly killed me
because I wanted to leave him; and once planning to use it in

retaliation against a man who'd beaten me because he didn't like what I'd said regarding our night out together. I very often attracted the macho type of men who didn't like a dose of their own medicine. That *I* would want to leave *them* was not allowed, and they would turn vicious. I had also been involved in dangerous incidents in the days when I had been prostituting. On many occasions only my razor-sharp cunning, a product of a powerful survival instinct, had saved me from being murdered. (For instance, I was to read in the newspapers one day that a man whom I had got away from by the skin of my teeth was later known to be a killer who had murdered several prostitutes.) So, thinking about all this, I decided that I would have to discover the way to cease relating to thug-type men and to find a way through all the barriers that were preventing me from getting happily close to a man. I told myself, 'You've got to stop escaping into gaol to hide away from it all. You've got to go forward into the struggle and come out on the other side.' Then it became a challenge to me.

For the first few months Christina had a very conventional and attractive sexual mate, Jean-Pierre, a young and wealthy Swiss student studying commercial English. Christina was leading a respectable life but the conventional rewards did not follow. She wanted her children to live with her but was told that she had no chance of getting council accommodation. In these circumstances, when Jean-Pierre (predictably) gave voice to a very romanticized and conventional view of children, Christina's logic, born of an exasperation at the world's hypocrisy, sliced off the superficial layers of his world in a way which he could not understand.

On previous occasions when I had been released from prison I had used my thieving money to get a flat for my children. Now that I had turned my back on crime I went to see a council accommodation worker with a view to getting a council flat. I was told by this official that I could expect to get a flat by the time my daughter's grandchildren had grown up. I had no reason to disbelieve him since I'd had nothing to do with that sort of thing before. I realized then that my children would have to stay in a Home until I was able to earn good money. I had a job waitressing at the time. Then, one day, Jean-Pierre said to me, 'Do you like children, Christina?' I said, 'Which children?' 'All children, Christina.' 'No', I said, 'I'm sure I don't, do you?' He looked shocked. 'Look', I said, 'See that expensive car you've got out there? (he had a Lotus Europa). The money you'd get from selling that would stop a lot of children from dying of starvation in India.' 'Oh,' he said, 'But India's a long way off.' 'Okay, let's forget about India, think instead about the slums in Naples.' He said, 'If only I could explain it to you in German.' That summed it up! People were coming at me left, right and centre for being the sort of person who had been a criminal and whose children were in a Home, but when I turned the argument in a way which showed them that they were fooling themselves, they didn't like it at all. And, of course, everyone has their justifications for their conventional ways of breaking the law (as in stealing from workplaces, fiddling expense accounts, etc.), right through the social spectrum. It was all very bewildering to me.

The Swiss student was not the only person whose language Christina did not speak. As she moved from one circle of people to another|she felt her marginal status more and more. She had rejected any notion that she had a fixed personality (schizophrenic, psychopathic or whatever!) and had accepted Dr. P.'s suggestion that she could become her own woman. Yet, having rejected, also, two of the major elements of her previous identity which had been mainly rooted in crime and an unsatisfying mode of socio-sexual interaction with men, Christina felt bereft of any|stable biographical bearings in which to anchor the constitutive elements of a new personality. 'I wanted to pass through the barriers of my social conditioning and thereby free my underlying real-self.' Part of the problem, also, was that Christina was an outsider with an insider knowledge. For whereas insiders seldom have outsider knowledge, outsiders always have insider knowledge. Remember that Christina, as a young teenager, had seen the man beneath the dog collar!

In that first year out of prison Christina became a waitress, a film extra and a model. She had assumed that men in film and modelling agencies would be able to see her as an interesting person rather than as a sex object.

I had no intentions of substituting a life of crime for a life of sexual exploitation. So my resolutions began to waver as soon as I went into film work and modelling and came across the first barrier with men which I couldn't handle. Yes, *I* could work, but *they* wanted sex. One way or another it was made quite explicit. One man summed it up for all the rest when he said, 'Thousands of good-looking women want to be models. We'd have to be idiots not to pick the ones we can have sex with.' I was devastated by this brick wall of an ultimatum and became very depressed. I went under the covers for a whole weekend, and I wept. 'What am I going to do?' I wondered. It seemed to me, then, that this was the kind of world that deserved the criminals it got. For a while I debated going back to my old way of life. But in those early days my resolution was still strong enough to overrule the adversity it encountered. Instead of going back to crime I told myself 'You've got to do the opposite. You've got to go into a world where it's not your looks that count. After all, supposing you were ugly, what then? You'd have to use your brains and your hands like most people do anyway.' It seemed to me that the kind of job I needed was one where I would be respected even though I was a woman, one where I could feel that I was doing something really worthwhile, and, most importantly, one where sex would not be an expected condition of the job. What about nursing?

Christina — Nurse, Mother, Shoplifter and Playmate

Christina, feeling oppressed in the so-called 'straight' society, yet still resolved not to engage in lawbreaking, now decided to construct her own prison-in-the-world. Nursing would not only provide economic security, respectability and safe accommodation, it would also give her, as a woman, a Madonna-like status. Once more she was grasping at an idealization of womanhood — this time the idealization of nurse as the representation of goodness. But, though nursing might provide remedies for some of her immediate needs, it could not remedy her more deep-rooted problems. For she continued to feel the ties of motherhood, continued to engage in personal relationships which had to be worked at, and was still saddled with an intellect which refused to paper over hypocrisy. Becoming a nurse would not prove to be her salvation. Rather it would mean that when she next achieved superwoman status she would be dancing to a different, though much more intricate, tune.

The more I questioned the pros and cons of becoming a nurse, the more such a move seemed tailor-made to my needs. It was imperative that I do a job which had a darn sight more meaning than just monetary gain. For even with the best of sociable intentions on my part, to become a wage-slave instead of being a thief seemed like one of those heads-you-win-tails-I-lose situations. Added to that, the amount of money I could expect to earn in an ordinary job — especially as a woman — seemed a pathetically insulting amount to me. To compensate for this (as well as to compensate for being made subject to an employer's requirements for most of each week) I knew that even though I couldn't expect to have an exciting job I must have a job which felt sufficiently worth doing for its own sake. Nursing the sick fulfilled this criterion. Secondly, I assumed that the hospital workplace would not pose any sexual problems with men and that life in a Nurses' Home, with no men allowed in, would in itself make life far easier for me. I could still carry on meeting men socially, but I could also withdraw from them into my nurse's room — my own little cell-in-the-world — whenever I felt the need to. Thirdly, seeing as I was down on record as being a baddy, by becoming a nurse I would set the record straight. After all, even at my worst I wasn't *only* Humphrey Bogart; I was always Shirley Temple too!

So I went to a hospital in Croydon for SRN training. They did not ask me if I had a police record and, as I had obtained the necessary O levels whilst on that eighteen-months juvenile sentence, I was accepted and became a probationer. If I had known what I was letting myself in for I would never have gone there at all. If I had believed in God I would have said that it had been sent as a penance — I came up against the pecking-order with a capital P. Not even the screws would have been as rude and ill-mannered as those sisters were! No one before had ever spoken to me the way they did and got away with it. I marvelled at my own self-control. I was often on the verge of telling them to fuck-off. Consultants, of course, were gods! There were exceptions — a few of the staff warmed my heart and I wished that I could be as lovely as they were. As for the patients, some of them reminded me of recidivist prisoners; they were all wrapped up inside the pettiest details of the institutional routine and everyone in it. Some bore suffering more terrible than I had ever previously imagined with a stoicism that I could only marvel at. As a nurse I saw disease and disability ravaging the human frame in ways that shocked and horrified me.

Christina found that many of the young nurses were religious and unbearably self-righteous. It came as a shock to her when she realized that they were not being hypocritical, that they really believed that their world view was the one and only correct one. At the mundane level, Christina also had little in common with them. Cliff Richard was their idol, the world was divided into the good and the bad, and they had predictably conventional views on almost every subject. When Christina started to have her children staying with her for the odd night, the other nurses complained that it was embarrassing to have a twelve-year-old male running round the place! At the end of that first year she was aged thirty-three. Given her feelings of mental estrangement from the other probationers, together with the fact that it was only for the first year that trainee nurses were required to live-in, it was not surprising that Christina decided to look round for her own accommodation so that she could have her children to stay with her overnight. Her determination to become a qualified nurse had not weakened and she was still studying hard. Unfortunately, however, the superwoman syndrome was being set in motion again, and with the same disastrous effects.

Outside the hospital I was still struggling in my relationships with men. Also I would have the children staying with me whenever I could, and, as I was coming up to my last year of training, I was studying very hard. As you can imagine, nursing took a lot out of me, both physically and mentally. Yet sometimes, like a fool, I would be out all night gallivanting in the sexual arena of clubland. Then I would return home, have a bath, put on my uniform and be on duty all day. But equally I would spend many evenings not going anywhere, just studying. When two of the nurses started to complain about my son being in the hostel, I decided to look for a place of my own, but it proved impossible to find a place which I could afford and where my two children would be allowed.

Eventually, I *did* settle for a place. I wanted so much to have the place that I took it even though the rent was as much as the whole of my nursing wage. That same old 'blind spot' began to work in me again. I was losing a grip on my common sense. I told myself that it would be OK to steal just enough to pay the rent. All I had to do was steal one item per week from one of the big stores — say a leather coat. I very soon learnt that I could not stop there. My rationalization was: 'Well, while I'm here, I might as well steal two things to save me coming back again next week.' But it didn't stop there either. Next it was, 'Well, it's daft not to take what I can whilst I'm here.' I have since realized that I was overestimating my capacity to control my own weakness. It was the same as when an alcoholic takes that second drink. The stealing just snow-balled.

Christina was working hard, playing hard. She spent her money on herself and her children and on ensuring that she could always pay her way socially in the pubs and the clubs. For she had realized that she could only expect to have an equal relationship with men if she were always seen to be financially independent of them. She had come to believe that even to let them pay for her social pleasures led them to expect a sexual response which she did not wish to feel obligated to give. If she were fair with them, she reasoned, they should be fair with her. During that time as a student nurse she had a couple of sexual friendships with men. She bought a car to ease her whirlwind round of full-time work, mothering, socializing and stealing. And she managed to enter the third and final year of her training before she was arrested.

I remember how at that time I often thought of myself as 'healing hands, stealing hands', and I also remember feeling more and more on top of things again, in that all-powerful way which I had known before. But something had to give, and it did. I got arrested for a whole load of stuff from Harrods — over a thousand pounds' worth. I remember letting out this blood-curdling scream when the store detectives jumped me. I thought I'd never stop screaming.

The hospital matron, who had a high regard for Christina's nursing ability, provided a good report for the court. Her ex-prison visitor, who had become a good friend, even spoke to the judge on her behalf. Christina was remanded to prison for two weeks for reports and when the case came to court she actually had two good psychiatric reports, one from the prison psychiatrist and one from her old friend Dr. P. The eventual outcome was to be a two-year suspended sentence. But Christina had been asked to resign temporarily from the hospital for the year prior to the trial and felt that she was in limbo again during that time. She moved from place to place until the court hearing and then, even though the Matron had invited her back to the hospital to continue her training, was told when she reported for duty that, because the case had got into the papers, the hospital Board of Visitors had insisted that she not be reinstated. Life appeared bleak.

I went into a decline. I got an all-night cleaning job and I felt a failure — mean and dirty. I looked as bad as I felt and during that time, for the first time in my life, men never gave me even *one* look — let alone a second! At first I felt pleased about that — it represented freedom from the advances of the predatory male whom I had originally been in moral danger of encountering! But after a few months I realized that it also represented a state of mind which would prevent me from ever again having the opportunity to enter into any satisfactory sexual friendship whatsoever. This worried me. I did still want to have a choice in the matter.

I did return to the Croydon Hospital as an auxiliary nurse two years after I had left there. I still looked awful. It wasn't until I was leaving the hospital, ten months later, that the nurses told me how, when they'd first seen me on my return there, they had thought I must be dying of cancer because I looked so appalling. That's how I looked and that's how I felt!

And still Christina felt that she had to fulfil her maternal obligations! Within a year, and prior to returning to nursing, she had, with the help of a social worker and two headmasters, succeeded in obtaining council accommodation and in getting her children back with her. Her son was fifteen, her daughter thirteen.

> I must admit that I didn't even remotely anticipate just how problematical the situation was going to be. They were now teenagers. Their extremely unsettled background and my unresolved inner conflicts caused all hell to be let loose between us. But at the time it had seemed like a valuable thing to do. Although they were taking their angry and confused feelings out on me, at least I was protecting them from Borstal, prison etc. I couldn't let them fall into the hands of the law-enforcement authorities. I didn't want history to repeat itself.

Back at the hospital, Christina found that although she had been taken on as an auxiliary nurse, she was, none the less, often doing the work of a much more experienced nurse. Yet, when she requested that she be allowed to complete her SRN training she was told that she would never be allowed to resume her training at that particular hospital. What had happened was that since the time of Christina's court case there had been a change of staff; a new matron had been promoted and a new chief tutor had arrived at the hospital. The new matron, who had known Christina previously, had in principle been sympathetic to her and had directed that a report on her work be made to the chief tutor, who would then decide whether or not she could resume her training. According to Christina, the report on her work was excellent, but none the less, the chief tutor claimed that she 'could not take the responsibility' for re-admitting her to the course. So Christina's application was turned down.

She left the Croydon hospital and decided to concentrate on being a full-time mother, but her children were becoming increasingly difficult to control. Once they had reached the age when they could live on their own without threat of being taken into care, therefore, Christina, feeling that she could do no more for them in the role of full-time mother, turned her thoughts once again to ways and means of establishing herself in a legitimate and worthwhile career. Conscious that she was nearing forty and thinking that the time to begin again as a trainee nurse might soon be past, it was with an even greater urgency that she renewed the struggle to gain entry to a hospital. Fortunately for her she was not entirely bereft of support. Through the good offices of both her friend the ex-prison visitor and an ex-Holloway prison matron, Christina finally managed to train and qualify as a State Enrolled Nurse at an orthopaedic hospital on the outskirts of London. Once qualified, she did agency nursing for a few months. Meanwhile ... further blows. First, her father died. Then, she experienced the final paternal rejection — father had disinherited her and left everything to her brother. Christina did her best to suppress the conflicting and painful feelings that ensued but discovered that she could no longer fulfil her own nursing standards. As she had already observed that nurses who had problems of their own could slip into taking it out on the patients, she knew that it was time to stop nursing when she found that she herself was becoming resentful of the patients' demands. Again she was overcome by depression. She remained unemployed and almost totally withdrawn from the world, and, for a while, could think of nothing that might attract her back into circulation. Then, after a week spent alone in trance-like introspection she decided to join a gestalt therapy group. After a few sessions she felt strong enough to enter the conventional world of work once more.

I went to college to study office practice, communications and audio typing. Six months, five days a week. I found it difficult but I managed to hold on. I passed all my exams but one and I got distinctions in those I did pass. Being a beginner at my age, I was so worried that I might not get a job that I snapped up the first offer that came along. It was a Chartered Accountants in High Street, Kensington, and I had to travel from Wood Green. I disliked the male dominance in the office. It was not sexual harrassment, but a pervasive air of sexism and exploitation that I didn't like. For instance, they didn't like it if you came in ten minutes late in the morning, but in the evening I was frequently kept back for half an hour, or even an hour, because letters were handed to me too late to be able to get them done during the correct working hours. It was expected that one would just stay and finish them. The rest of the employees agreed that it wasn't fair, but then would add, 'Oh, but they give us a good bonus at Christmas.' I have worked in thirteen different jobs since my last prison sentence and I have never ceased to be amazed at the amount of unfairness employees feel both obligated to put up with and compelled to rationalize away. I've always needed to feel that I was being treated fairly as I went along. But I have also noted that employees get their own back on the employers in underhand ways. Understandably. Even so, having to work in that kind of atmosphere gets me down. As far as I'm concerned I'd sooner have less money than be exploited. So, feeling sick of it all, I decided I'd give myself a complete change of environment. Within four weeks I had sold what I could to get both the fare to Rome and enough money for a month's board and lodging when I got there. With two suitcases, one hold-all and all my paintings — the total sum of all my worldly goods — I arrived in Rome a couple of weeks or so before Christmas 1980.

In Rome Christina was to all appearances successful. At first she had a short-lived job as a chauffeuse/nanny which she left when she discovered after taking up the post that she had been misled as to the terms of the appointment. She was in fact expected to work an eighty-hour week! She then managed to obtain a full-time post teaching English in a school. This post turned out to be even better than she had at first realized. For the school had a contract to teach English at the University and, accordingly, on two days a week she had to give lectures at the Universita Gregoriana situated in the centre of Rome. Christina had become Professora! Furthermore, a rich and decent man wanted to marry her.

Everyone I met was saying that I was the luckiest woman in Rome, that other women in my position just had to put up with au-pair work. Also, Allan wanted to marry me and friends were saying that at my age I would be mad not to jump at the chance of such a catch. I must admit that I was tempted. But all the good reasons for marrying Allan were cancelled out by the thought of years of intimacy with a man with whom I was not even remotely in love. I was well aware that I was lucky and on a superficial level I was feeling good, but I was also having a psychosomatic reaction to the whole adventure. Altogether I was there three months and right from the beginning I had this psychosomatic reaction — even though I seemed to all intents and appearances to have landed on my feet. After all I had never been to Rome before, and knew no one who lived there either, yet within a couple of weeks I was working in a top-status position, being courted by a wealthy and well-liked man and was surrounded by a circle of admiring and pleasantly flattering people. Despite all this, nearly everything that could go wrong with one's respiratory tract went wrong with mine — and the final straw was when loss of my voice made teaching impossible! Added to this, I was feeling weaker and weaker until it came to the point when even standing up resulted in giddiness. I took myself to bed and lay there reviewing both the immediate situation and the whole of my life so far. Something was vitally wrong. Once again I felt defeated. Ever since I had tried to stop leading a criminal life and make a new life for myself, it had felt as if there were a giant octopus — the one that I mentioned earlier — in my way. How could I explain this Sisyphean-like trap I seemed to be in? I seemed to have proved to myself that I couldn't be a nurse, that I couldn't be a secretary, that I couldn't be a teacher and that I couldn't even be a sugar-daddy's wife either! Surely, then it must mean that I should go back to being the criminal that I used to be!

Christina felt confused and defeated. Additionally, she was filled with guilt at the discovery that her inner needs were not even to be satisfied by the outward and conventional symbols of success. She felt powerless to influence her own destiny any more. Then she panicked. If the conventional symbols of successful respectability did not satisfy the inner self then, she reasoned, that inner self must be essentially deviant — in her own case, a born thief. For a time therefore, she abandoned her earlier rejections of the notion of 'fixed personality' and instead, indulged what she then believed to be the essential thief in her. She returned to shoplifting with a vengeance. A series of arrests and court appearances followed, interspersed with very short periods of nursing and promiscuous, often violent, relationships with men.

I was rapidly going downhill but every so often I would stop, take stock of myself and try to halt the process by going back to nursing. Then, very quickly, I would realize that I was in no fit state to nurse, give it up, and begin stealing again . . . worse than before! The final irony was realizing that I was in no fit state to be a thief either. The days when I had been a sophisticated thief were the days when I had done my thieving with a sense of triumph at getting back at a society that had initially attacked me. Now I was thieving with a sense of despair, feeling myself to be nothing but a failure and a loser. Realizing this — and at the same time suffering from a sense of defeat in my struggle to succeed in relating well with a man — I began to believe that it wasn't thieving that was my natural bent, it was being a gaol-bird that was my natural disposition. After all, hadn't I spent nine and a half years in gaol by the time I had just turned thirty-one? I began then to have visions of landing in a cell in isolation in prison and of spending the rest of my days there — curled up in a little ball and immersed in dreaming fantasies. The vision both attracted me and repelled me. I experienced it both as a way of getting away from an unbearable world and as an asylum for a defeated deviant self, a self lost to the world. In my desperation I was as good as asking to be caught. (I couldn't bear actually to ask to go to prison straight out, but I came very close.) I was half hoping to force someone to see what a shocking state I was in even though I didn't see what earthly good that could do. Luckily for me, at this time probation officers came to my rescue over and over again, always writing out supportive reports for the magistrates to read. Equally, and I have to admit it, magistrates seemed determined to keep me out of prison. I was lucky, but also I was putting up a tremendous fight against my own wilful descent into self-destruction. I went from suspended sentence to probation to day-training-centre one after the other. I was also frantically picking up men and then realizing that I didn't want them. More trouble, since the kind of men whom I was associating with then were the kind of men who thought that they owned you after they had had sex with you even once.

After skipping bail to run off to Amsterdam with a man whom she had met in a bail hostel where she had been living under a Court Order, Christina realized that she had had enough. She voluntarily returned to England, gave herself up and fully expected to be sent straight to prison. Instead, to everyone's astonishment, the magistrate seemed determined to inhibit her apparent urge to self-destruct. Christina was given a conditional discharge which she received with very mixed feelings indeed. Prison would at least have given her a temporary refuge from what she was now experiencing as absolutely insurmountable problems. Instead, here she was being given a chance to review the situation yet again! For the first time in her life she went voluntarily to live in a probation hostel. In the non-authoritarian and supportive regime of that particular hostel it finally came home to Christina that she must halt the search for external success until she had come to understand the social conditioning of her own inner existence.

Christina — In her own Time

Today, nine months after leaving that hostel, Christina is living alone in her own bed-sitter flat, but she has not rushed into any new working situations. Indeed, she is nowadays careful to avoid any situations which might make her either mentally or physically ill. Although she still has the vitality to try anything which she thinks may be creative, she is becoming quicker at spotting the danger signals. Aware of the way in which she has for so long attempted both to surpass and reject all the competing definitions of womanhood which have assailed her, Christina is now attempting to lie fallow. She has realized that in her desperate attempts to avoid being a clockwork person she has, for much of the time, merely become an anti-clockwork person.

It has not proved possible to overcome the barriers which prevent my daughter, my son and me from being close. After many years of struggling to succeed in this aim I have recently felt obliged to admit defeat; indeed, I had even begun to fear that I might go under if I remained in that struggle. And although I now feel relieved that I have made this decision, I also feel very saddened and bewildered that it had to come to this.

As for a sexual mate, I left the last one in Amsterdam sixteen months ago. He was the one I got on with best of all. So far, overall, it seems to me that I prefer celibacy so at the moment I'm choosing to remain solo. That said, I still look forward to the day when I can share a deep love with a man. But gone are the days when I could mistakenly enter into a sexual relationship about which I was only half-hearted and then think that all the onus was on me to make it work. Such propositions I now gracefully decline.

So, here I am living on the dole, just about managing to live on the paltry amount of money that entails. But I'm not complaining. On the contrary. I am glad to have the opportunity to work out the rhythms of my own inner orchestration without external demands being made on me. Much as I would prefer more money, it could not compensate me for the loss of this opportunity. I can't help smiling though, when I remember that nearly forty years ago as a thieving child, I had just about the same amount per week to spend on playtime as I now have per week to spend on food, electricity and gas bills, cleaning materials, sanitary towels and other such necessities. Then, also, I think of the times when I was averaging six-hundred pounds a week as a thief in the sixties, during my free years. Learning how to be a pauper without feeling resentfully deprived or humiliated has been another powerful struggle. But I've succeeded, I'm happy to say — and I could write a book on that theme alone!

I am lucky in that my health, intelligence and looks have not deserted me. People usually take to me easily. Also, I feel that I am gaining tremendously from the ways in which I am now perceiving the multi-faceted variety of experiences that I have lived through. Too often I have been struggling against my own grain. In the days when I was a full-time thief I felt upright and strong. It was a strength born of outrage and fed on arrogance. Since my last prison sentence I've had my fall from those heights. I've had to eat humble pie and I've hated it. But it's well digested now and it has ceased to nauseate me. As I now stand, I don't feel upright and strong, but neither do I feel freakish and powerless any more, thank goodness.

What I have written in this chapter is a skeletal view of myself compared to the full-bodied autobiography which I am planning to embark on next. It was whilst concentrating on writing this chapter as honestly as memory permits and bearing in mind that I must protect others from exposure and myself from repercussions, that I became aware for the first time of an area in myself which I have so far managed to keep hidden from my own view. It seems to me that I have hit on Jung's 'shadow side' and, using the afore-mentioned autobiography as the means, I now intend to scrutinize this deep dark area of myself. I hope that by bringing this area to consciousness I'll at last effect a true integration. I'm not expecting to be able to rush this process along. I *am* hoping that with a bit of luck I may have another forty-seven years of life ahead of me, and that this time, I'll succeed in making some of my dreams come true . . . With that scarey but exciting thought, I say farewell.

That is Christina's story. We have neither justified it nor romanticized it. Rather, in deconstructing Christina's career we have merely tried to present an alternative history, one which has attempted to lay bare some of the ideological contradictions which condition prevailing and dominant images of womanhood. Not all women respond by breaking the law but, as we also saw in chapter one, criminal activity can provide, at least in the short term, one satisfying alternative to the frustrations of conventional womanhood. So in deconstructing Christina's particular story we have not so much attempted to explain *why* she took the path she did. Rather we have tried to show under what conditions a criminal response can be possible, rational and to some degree satisfying. In other words, our alternative history makes sense of a career which, when presented in official records and reports, might appear to make no sense at all.

Christina alone has to put the pieces back together. She knows that this time it will have to be different. Not again will she dance to the tunes of Others. Already she has paid the piper, now she will call the tune . . . but she will do it in her own *good* time.

3
Jenny: In a Criminal Business

Jenny Hicks and Pat Carlen

Introduction

Imbued with the spirit of the entrepreneur and encouraged
by my adoptive right-wing working-class mother to be
ambitious, I was an organizer of events from a very early age.
Looking back now I can see also that to date my life has been
more or less organized around two dominant desires: to be
creative in my dealings with the world around me; and to be
constructively independent in my own development as a
person. At various stages in my life these desires have been
realized in completely different forms, but when in 1964 I
adopted both the philosophy of maximum profit for personal
gain and the role of employer in the capitalist business world
my creativity took a criminal form. In no time at all the very
thin line between legitimate and illegitimate business practices
became blurred. I soon slipped over that line and became
equal partner in a fraud that was successful for at least ten
years. In this chapter we shall describe and comment on my
life from May 1939 when I was born to a single Irish woman
living in London's Marylebone Road workhouse to June 1976
when I was convicted at the Old Bailey for conspiring to
defraud the GPO of a quarter-of-a-million pounds.

Family Business

I was never a naughty girl. I have asked around for other
opinions and the consensus seems to be that I was a placid,
well-behaved, sensible, outgoing and friendly child, young
woman and woman.

I do not remember having to suppress any desires to be

naughty either, although as with most kids there was the odd occasion when I was. For instance, when I was barely able to see over the top of the old-fashioned grocer's counter I was filled with a desire to pop a small bit of the cheese in my mouth. As quickly as the desire came so did its antidote. I was overcome with shame and appalled by my wicked thought. So much for my naughtiness!

Where this sense of morality and accepted standards of good behaviour came from is unclear. Neither of my Mothers (I have two and will explain this later) says that she can remember having to spell out to me what things were done and not done. Apparently I sorted this out for myself. Mother Lena says that it is an inherited wisdom, whilst Mother Hicks believes that it was due to the example she set. As for me I would not claim to know, though I do think that we test the limits of accepted behaviour with childish initiatives that are either checked by disapproval or unchecked by encouragement. I took the normal 'testing' initiatives but always, as far as I can recall, after weighing up with cautious consideration their chances of success; and my gauge of success was adult approval. For my part, I certainly cannot remember having any sense of injustice, inequality or social hypocrisy. At that time I wasn't, in fact, aware of anything which might have led me to question the conventional standards of morality or behaviour. Mother Hicks remembers that, 'you always wanted your own way', adding ruefully, 'and you always got it'. When she is pressed to clarify why I got my own way and others did not she confirms that I was always 'so sensible about it'. It seems that my good sense steered me through my childhood. Whether my morality was inherited from my natural mother or inculcated by my adoptive mother remains unclear.

So how did this very good little girl end up some thirty-six years later at the Old Bailey convicted of defrauding the GPO of a quarter-of-a-million pounds? And how could I commit such an offence with the greatest ease and without disturbing my own sense of logic and morality?

Perhaps, at this point, I should explain why I had two Mothers. First there was Lena who gave birth to me on 4 May 1939 in the workhouse in London's Marylebone Road. Half Irish and half Scots, Lena was born in Leitrum just south of the border in Ireland. My Great-granny was a fearless little woman and Catholic through and through, so Catholic in fact that she declared that if she found one little bit of Protestant in her body she would cut it out! Lena was consistently beaten for dancing with the Orangemen's Parade and Great-granny was feared by both armed and unarmed Provos. The day the armed and hooded Provos came to take one of her sons who had refused to join up, Great-granny beat them off and ran up the street waving her stick with one hand and clutching her three-cornered black shawl with the other. Great-granny was a force to be reckoned with! Grandfather, on the other hand, contributed little to the family but harrassment and aggression. He died in 1918.

Born and reared in Ireland Lena eventually left to work in service in England. At that time, domestic service was the only occupation open to women with no connections or references, no matter how intelligent or capable they might have been. The social order in England was shifting along with the economy. Industry was drawing its work-force from a feudal countryside, rural and urban life was dividing and the post-Edwardian prosperity was changing hands and going to newer, more entrepreneurial, families. As a result of this shift, many of the 'older' families found themselves slipping down the social scale. Used to a| lifestyle which depended upon an army of servants which they could no longer afford, these families made the remaining few servants work like slaves. Lena was, more often than not, expected to do the work of six people. The post which she had at the time of her pregnancy was typical. Her work included: lighting all the open fires; cleaning the entire house; taking early-morning tea to her employers; cooking, serving and washing-up after breakfast, lunch, tea and dinner; and washing, starching and pressing all the clothes. For all this she received three pounds a month. How she found the time to become pregnant I shall never know. It did not seem important to know who my father is — or was. I never asked, and I still do not know. Much more relevant to my story is my other mother, Mother Hicks.

Once she was pregnant, Lena moved to a household in Kensington. This time her employers, a sympathetic Jewish family, did not work her to death and the kindly lady of the house asked her if she was pregnant. Lena, being both independent and proud, denied her pregnancy and took off with a bulging tummy to the workhouse. It was there, cleaning the stone steps and searching the dustbins for crusts of bread, that Lena spent the last few weeks of her confinement.

In 1939, when I was born at St. Mary's Hospital Paddington, Britain was on the brink of war and I was born into the least privileged stratum of an unequal society. The odds were pretty much stacked against Lena and me! Yet, despite the odds, I was a placid, quiet and contented baby. It was only a short time after my birth that we were evacuated from Marylebone to a village in Surrey where Lena took a job in a munitions factory during the day and worked in a nursing home at night. She soon realized, however, that, even working all those hours, she would never be able to afford to keep me. She was also unhappy with the woman who looked after me whilst she was at work. Resourceful and independent as ever, Lena rejected the usual adoption agencies and advertised for foster parents in the local newspaper. This method ensured that she could foster me on her own terms *and* negotiate access. This would have been impossible through the normal adoption channels. So Mother and Father Hicks were found and vetted, and, after a trial run, Lena agreed to them legally adopting me. She was sure that they adored, if not worshipped, me! She particularly delighted in the way my new Dad ironed my cot sheets to warm them before bedtime!

Memories of this time are fleeting. I do remember beginning to stand before the two women: one proudly showing the other my progress, the other sitting on the edge of her chair eager and proud of my endeavours. Lena had, in fact, chosen well. My new parents loved each other and they loved me too.

I was always aware of Mother Hicks's ambitions. She admired people who 'got on in life'. She also admired hard work, but you could get away without the hard work if you 'got on' and had the right connections. But Mother Hicks herself never got away without a great deal of hard work. She kept the house, doing everything and expecting nothing from me in the way of chores except a little shopping on Saturdays.

She also had a part time job to supplement the family finances. I did not question the amount of work done by Mother Hicks and, with Lena visiting us regularly, I passed through a warm and loving childhood. It might even have been said that I was a little spoiled from all sides.

I started school when I was six years old and I soon learned that life would not be worth living unless I passed the eleven-plus. Mother made this very clear and, as she gave me so much and I gave her so little, I thought that the least I could do was to get a scholarship. Dad and Lena did not seem to mind whether I passed or not, but all were delighted when I did. I, too, was pleased, because the more I learned about the alternative to the grammar school, the less I liked the prospect. It seemed a very rough place and lots of fights took place within it. I hated rough behaviour then and I still do. It is not so much that it scares me, rather that violence upsets me, and particularly if it involves women.

We chose a coeducational grammar school and Mother Hicks felt that from now on I would be on the right road and that everything else would fall into place. I joined the Girl Guides, took 'cello lessons, attended Methodist meetings, and was a member of many school societies. Once again, 'you name it, Jenny Hicks was in it!'

I cottoned on quite early to the fact that Mother Hicks had a somewhat Victorian attitude towards sex. It was a rigid and disapproving view which I did not share. As soon as sexual feelings entered my life at the age of seven or eight I decided that this side of me was to be kept a secret. Sex was something personal that belonged only to me and whoever I was involved with at the moment. Intuitively I knew that if Mother Hicks became aware of this part of me she would set out to destroy it; and I thought that others would too. My desire for secrecy in my sexual and love-life remains. Perhaps it is a response to that early intimation that my sexual orientation would somehow not be considered normal. But it all seemed perfectly natural to *me* and no one who would have disapproved found out. In my own book I was still being a 'good girl' and that was all that mattered. But one upsetting process always seemed to happen — my best girl friends always left me eventually and went off with one of the boys!

Not that I had anything against boys, some of my best friends were boys! Tony for instance, was a mate who lived around the corner and we had great times together. I got on well with his mates too, but they just were not as exciting and interesting as the girls whom I knew. Yet since, one after another, my girl friends deserted me for one of these boring boys, I thought that I had better check out what on earth it was about boys that interested girls so much. I kissed one or two and one of them showed me his penis. I felt very sorry for him being stuck with something so ugly and offensive but I was even more appalled that my girl friends could leave me for that. The boy—girl syndrome was just too ridiculous for me to consider it as a serious staging-post to adulthood.

Tony once told me that, no matter what, he would end up like his Dad. I could not see why he had to and I told him so. He was a talented artist and musician, why should he follow the same path as his parents? I stressed the alternatives that there were for him, but he was adamant — he would end up working on the railways, or something similar, with a wife and kids . . . just like his Dad He said that he knew that I would 'get out' — but not him. I could not understand the deterministic fatalism of this attitude but, even then, I knew that he was right. I had always known that I would not marry — and I did get out.

Like Chris (chapter one), Jenny did not find school stimulating. Her teachers discouraged her tentative inquiries about University and, in general, education was presented as a grind, a reward for the privileged few who had connections, stamina and education but certainly not within the realms of possibility for a working-class girl. And, like most working-class girls then (and now) Jenny accepted her teachers' evaluation of her chances of educational success. She was a sociable, active and creative pupil — but the mysteries of the educational system seemed beyond comprehension, and in any case, were they worth fathoming, if her own teachers were typical examples of the end-product? So Jenny put most of her energies into out-of-school activities and she quickly discovered that she had an entrepreneurial flair.

I enjoyed organizing group activities: dog shows, jumble

sales, arts and crafts exhibitions, fancy-dress shows, talent competitions etc. None of these were money-making activities. Mother Hicks would never admit that we were poor and she disapproved both of us raising money for charitable organizations and of us making money for ourselves. I was, in fact, brought up in a law-abiding family with strict morals about the handling of money.

More Exciting Business

Childhood had been a happy time. With the onset of adolescence, clouds began to loom. Girl friends paired off with boys — and vice-versa. It was the end of all fun. By the age of fourteen, I was beginning to find fault with the parochial world with which I had previously been so satisfied. I began to look further afield and to look also at some of the other worlds which, largely through the newspapers, were beginning to impinge on mine. As chance would have it, the most exciting world seemed to be the just-beginning world of pop. It was 1953, Johnnie Ray was in town and I decided to join the hordes of teenagers who always met his plane at the airport. Looking back now from the vantage point of some thirty years on, I can see that I merely became involved in what appeared, at that time, to be the best experience on offer to a girl looking for a better life than the conventional one envisaged for her by teachers and parents. Ten years later it could have been CND — twenty years further on, and it could have been Greenham, or some other branch of the Women's Movement. It would certainly have been better for me if it had been. The Women's Movement allows for the personal and individual development of women and it provides a supportive structure within which women can develop both outside and apart from the traditional roles offered to them. But back in the fifties there wasn't much of anything. We were all just recovered from the war . . . and there was Johnnie Ray. In no time at all as I waited for that plane, I was transported into a different world. Chatting to different women, I heard talk of things I'd never previously dreamed of: seedy clubland, posh clubland and the glamorous London hotels — The Dorchester, The Mayfair and so on.

Here was an opportunity once more to organize, to be with women whose main concerns were definitely not marriage and motherhood.

It was the beginning of one of the happiest periods in Jenny's life. She formed her own Johnnie Ray Fan Club for the counties of Middlesex and Surrey and became a close friend of Marie who was already recognized as being a leading light amongst the Johnnie Ray fans. By the time she had left school, Jenny was immersed in the world of variety entertainment and she was spending most of her free time with Marie. It was a lifestyle which she was to enjoy for the next seven years. But it was a lifestyle which, to begin with at least, was absolutely law-abiding.

So I slipped out of school into another life. I started work at a local office earning two-pounds-fifty a week. To finance our visits to the Clubs when Johnnie Ray was in town, we got part-time jobs in addition to our full-time ones. We never thought of getting money in any way other than by earning it. For Marie and me, Johnnie Ray activities were definitely not inspired by the profit motive. We were completely 'pure' in our motivation and in our organization of the clubs, though not everyone was like us. Peter for instance, ran his club with an eye to profit and I met him soon after I met Marie. At that time, of course, I would never have predicted that one day I should stand beside him at the Old Bailey, accused of stealing a quarter of a million! Indeed, ironically, we first met when Marie summonsed him to tea to 'account' for his sharp practices! He was charming, but unrepentent. Peter was always a Capitalist with a capital C.

Life was full. It became even fuller when Jenny and Marie started up their first commercial enterprise, Bacchus Duplicating. Around this time, too, Jenny was introduced to speed — a necessary prop to a whirlwind life in which she and Marie were only taking a couple of hours' sleep a night. The intersecting worlds of commerce and drugs, however, were of a different order of morality and legality, to the innocent romanticism of a mid-fifties singer's fan club. Jenny was still innocent of any lawbreaking, but she began to have intimations of just how thin is the line between legality and illegality.

One night at a party we were complaining about our tiredness due to lack of sleep. When we said that we needed sleep so badly that we would have to leave the party early, a guy offered us some small white pills, saying, 'Take these when you wake up in the morning, and you'll be OK'. So next morning, two pills, coffee and on to the tube as usual — barely awake! Suddenly, the tube looked amazing. The adverts were interesting, the people fantastic and when I got to the office — wow! I worked like the clappers. That was it! From that time on I was to take speed on and off for many years. At that time Preludin could be bought over the counter in bottles of two-hundred-and-fifty. So there was still no lawbreaking either. Speed ensured that we lived every moment to the full in a world where our excitement was being constantly renewed.

We moved with many different people, and some of them were criminals. They used to discuss jobs and schemes in front of us and, though we never considered joining in any of their schemes, God alone knows how many times we could have been roped-in on a conspiracy charge. But I recognize all that only with the benefit of hindsight. At the time, I just assumed that I would be protected by my innocence — or was it my naivety? One night, for instance, we sat up drinking quite unconcernedly with friends who were waiting for what I now know to have been fourteen-years-in-prison-worth of heroin. But to me then it was all part of a scene through which I could move with impunity and there was always some exciting but legal scheme afoot to fulfil my need for action.

It was the beginning of the 'sixties and Bacchus Duplicating was expanding. After some debate, we decided to take on work for the Elvis Presley Fan Club. Next, after being assured that the enterprise was legal, we typed and printed for some fellows selling 'dirty' pictures. In fact, and again with hindsight, I would claim that the photos were definitely obscene, but as we had once been stopped and searched by the police whilst carrying some of these 'works of art' and as they had sent us on our way without comment, I remain ignorant to this day of their exact 'legal' status. Maybe it was in relation to those photos that I did first begin to realize that the Law's conception of right and wrong — as upheld in laws defining what is legal and illegal — had no one-to-one relationship with my own views of right and wrong, or, I suspect, many other people's. Certainly I became more cynical as I observed a series of events which to me smacked of hypocrisy, bigotry or just sheer mean-mindedness. First, prostitutes were driven off the street — but it was OK if their richer customers came to them in flats. Then Johnnie Ray was imprisoned — for homosexuality. Finally, the crunch — Preludin was taken off the market and could only be legally obtained by prescription. I asked my doctor to prescribe the pills for me but he refused. As I considered that I knew best what to put in my own body I decided to buy from the black market. At the stroke of a pen, the criminal law had turned me into a lawbreaker! Once we were dealing in the black market we bought in large quantities, and consumed in large quantities too. Our purchases became more varied. We bought Preludin, purple hearts, Benzedrine, Methedrine, Dexedrins and hashish. Heroin I balked at. The needle I could not take . . . though we bought one just in case. It was to be another twelve years, even, before I learned to enjoy hashish.

In the meantime Bacchus was making money, but as we did not register for tax we were, by now, committing two crimes. Though neither of our criminal activities worried us unduly, I had learned a useful lesson: that no great decisions were necessary to become criminal. One could just slip over from legality to illegality without any effort, without any change of lifestyle and, probably *because* of the two former conditions, without any debilitating sense of guilt. A certain amount of lawbreaking was almost a condition of living in the fast lane and, if it did not harm anyone else, why stop to worry about it?

Yet, just as it was easy to slip over the legal boundaries so, at this stage, was it comparatively easy to retreat once more to a legal position. Jenny and Marie did eventually decide to register their company, both for tax purposes and as a partnership. Indeed business was booming to such an extent that they had to make business trips to Paris — and were able to enjoy a lavish lifestyle whilst they were there. The end of their close relationship was in sight, however, strained maybe by the tensions of living and working so hard in such continuous and close proximity.

> Marie met Derek at work. She had never been seriously interested in anyone else before other than me but she wanted to have Derek around frequently. Consumed with jealousy, I hated him and behaved appallingly. She, of course, turned more and more to him. When her boss offered her a job as joint manager (with Derek) of a block of bed-sits she told me at once that she was going to take it.
>
> I was devastated. I walked out of that flat more miserable than I had ever been in my life. I left everything behind me. I went home to Mother Hicks. Dad had recently died and though I had been embittered by his death I was not really much of a comfort to Mother Hicks. I was too wrapped up in my own despair. The women I had known from the Johnnie Ray Clubs were, by this time, either married or engaged to be married. Although the fan clubs had provided us with immediate excitement they had not left us with any deeper satisfactions. They had given us neither a sense of individual or collective strength as women, nor had they developed us intellectually. We had poured all our energies and emotions into the media-inspired promotion of a male pop-star and were left, when the whole thing fizzled out, with a vacuum — wondering what it had all been about.

Serious Business/Criminal Business

For Jenny it was the end of an idyllic era. Her immediate task was to nurse her wounds and to make sure that when she next ventured forth her armour would be sufficient to guard her against further blows. Next time around, she would be more self-sufficient, less dependent upon personal relationships in her business life and more single-minded in her pursuit of financial gain and success. After four or five months she decided to visit Peter, the only person with whom she had kept in regular contact since she and Marie had split up.

Peter had a duplicating and mailing business similar to ours at Bacchus. Within four weeks of my visiting him, he asked me to go in with him as an equal assistant. I said 'OK, I want the rent to be paid on a flat locally; I want a regular wage in the bank; and, when I want to pull-out, I want the money to buy the equivalent of whatever we have at that time.' He agreed, and life with 'The Company' began. Officially, I was company secretary. I went in with Peter because I felt so lonely and isolated at home. But I was still on valium and I felt only half-alive. As soon as I began to work for him I realized that Peter wasn't too fussy about who his (our) clients were. For instance, I discovered straight away that we had a big order from a crooked company which offered people high returns on investments in pigs. It was the kind of company where investors seldom saw any returns and absolutely never received their cash back. I did demur over that one but Peter assured me that it was the very last order from the firm and — what the hell! — I just wanted to get on with it and get us into bigger and better business.

One of the first things I did was to advertise for homeworkers to address the envelopes. The response was phenomenal — hordes of women with kids queuing the whole length of the block all day. We offered rates of pay which were appalling and we took on fifty women and turned a hundred-and-fifty away. We were paying about one-sixth of what we had paid at Bacchus, we selected women who really needed the money and then we treated them absolutely callously. My concern for them as human beings was non-existent. I was an employer out to make the maximum profit and gain. The homeworkers had to give me their last drop of sweat and I gave them the fewest possible pennies in return for it. One slip and they were out. No excuses were allowed. Husband ill, kids ill, I couldn't have cared less. If the work wasn't returned on the day it was due, if it wasn't perfectly typed, then no more work and certainly no pay for the faulty batch. After all, there were hundreds more waiting at the gate. For me it was a way of life, a living. For them it was all that was on offer. For all of us it was the logical and rational end-product of the dominant capitalist ideology. I had been born into the same class and gender as the women I was now exploiting but if I could rise above the disabilities imposed by class and gender then this time I was going to — even if it meant climbing on their backs to do it.

My life was completely changing. Previously, personal relationships had been the most important factors in my life. Now I only cared about the business. I learned to drive and I bought a car. This gave me freedom and independence but apart from Peter, his friend and long drives out with Mother Hicks, my social life was almost non-existent.

Gradually things came together and at the end of the first year Peter and I looked at the books. What we saw was not encouraging. We had employed more people, taken on more customers but, somehow, we had not made that much money. We were definitely the poor relations of the advertising world. Direct Mail budgets[1] leave very little for work charges, and our profit percentages were not impressive. Out of every thousand pounds paid to us by our clients, nine-hundred went to the Post Office. Of the remaining hundred pounds we were lucky if we kept thirty for ourselves. I cannot remember which of us first thought about 'fixing' the franking machine but, before we got to thinking about that, we had already done most of the other accepted business fiddles.

There was the purchase tax, for instance. When the purchase-tax man came we sat him in a very cold little office near the open front door, turned off the heating and kept interrupting him while he was looking at the books. We didn't want him to look at the books too closely, and he didn't. He okayed them and went. The art was always to go just over the edge of legality or, better, to move the line just ever so slightly so that you could always claim innocence if anything did come to light. Same with the income tax; putting in for expenses that you hadn't actually had and so on. Insurance fraud was another fiddle. We had a carpet that had become worn and damp. If a pipe had burst we could have claimed on the insurance. But a pipe hadn't burst . . . so we organized a burst and the claim was successful. We were not so much thinking of engaging in frauds, but we had a business to run and there were certain things which could be done to ensure that we kept in business.

Rates were never paid until the bailiff came; we raised

capital by lying to the banks about contracts; and we paid all bills as late as we possibly could. Additionally, we became experienced at selecting the homeworkers whom we could most exploit. The ideal homeworker was someone who had been very proud of her job, was struggling economically and was presently tied down at home with her kids. Men made very poor homeworkers, though sometimes we would take on a gay man if he were very timid and obviously not going to be any trouble. The typists were usually not so badly-off as the enclosers. They tended to be much more lower class, often with their husbands out of work, and were just struggling to survive. Sometimes I would drive round in my car to check them out and there they'd be, often just in one room with all their kids around them. I didn't feel at all sorry for them, they just aggravated me when they didn't come up with the goods. Some grew to hate us and would come in and throw the envelopes at us, or bring them in and say that the cat had peed on them. All that I felt was irritation. They lost their jobs and we took on someone else. It was the same with the people whom we employed in the office. We always thought it best to play on the insecurities of those who couldn't get work, such as foreigners or black people, those who were timid and wanted to please, the 'yes' people. At the end of that first year, however, I really couldn't have cared less about the problems of the homeworkers or the other employees. Emotionally I was dead and conceived of success only in either financial or business terms. What was exercising my mind was how we could ever wring greater profits out of the business. It was obviously the postage which had to be looked at more closely.

A friend of Peter's had found an old hand franking-machine and had said that he could fix it so that they wouldn't know how much postage had been used. Not much use to us! A hand franking-machine wouldn't have been able to cope with the amount of mailing that we were doing. So, for the time being, we managed just through a man we knew at the Post Office. He would sort our letters into rebate areas; the postage on them would then be slightly cheaper and that was a saving which we didn't pass on to our clients. It was perfectly legal but it was a cumbersome method because we had to pay the man and, also, we had to have large enough amounts to be posted on the same day for it to be worthwhile. So my mind went back to the franking-machine.

Businesses and other large organizations use franking-machines to stamp their mail. You hire a meter on licence from the Post Office and you pay money into the Post Office. The amount of money to your credit is then registered in a sealed compartment in the meter. The seal is similar to the ones you find on electricity meters. When you pay money in at the Post Office they unseal it, register the amount and reseal it. A very simple operation. The meter is then fixed to a franking-machine and you can use up the money you've paid in. We already knew that it was easy enough to add to the amount of our registered credit fraudulently. The seals were very easy to unseal and reseal. But it was no use just adding money to the meter because you had a card marked with all the money you had put in and the Post Office were wise enough to keep a duplicate. There was no question of forging the card, therefore, unless you had help from the other side of the post office counter. Also there is an ascending register in the meter, which registers every item put through the meter and this number is *always* recorded on the card at the Post Office. This register was not so easy to get at. It was built into the meter and the screws around the casing had been burnt off. It seemed to us, therefore, that it was the ascending register that we had to go for. That ascending register became a challenge and we were both thinking round it when one day we hit the jackpot. We suddenly had the brilliant idea that maybe — just maybe — if we could get that ascending register to hit all the nines, then, as with a speedometer, it would go back to nought and we could then readjust it, thus cancelling out what we'd already had — including any extra we had put on ourselves — and begin again. One evening we took off the easy seal from the meter, took off the top of the franking machine, put through all the mail we had saved up for this moment — and then pushed through empty envelopes until the ascending register hit all the nines. When it reached that point . . . it went back to nought. Jackpot! It was a licence to print money. Gradually we refined the mechanics of the process. We were licensed at the Post Office in Victoria Street but we used to put our mail into the main sorting office at Howick Place. Our rebate sorting had already taught us a few lessons. We knew that if you sort your mail into areas and then post it at four in the afternoon when they're very busy, they'll just throw it onto the van that's going out. As far as Victoria Street was concerned we hadn't changed our usage on the machine at all because we still paid the same amounts to them. Howick Place, where we actually posted our rapidly increasing orders, had no check on our meter.

We both recognized that we were now into Crime with a capital C. There was no doubt about that! So we set into operation a few rules, one being that we always addressed an envelope to ourselves to ensure that the Post Office had not got wind of the operation and, as a consequence, was holding back our mail. Second, we decided that in future we could only take on customers who had a good reputation. Third, we both agreed that if you do commit a crime like this that it is best if the rest of your life is without blemish. Fourth, we would be the only ones in the secret — we would be the only ones who would ever do the franking.

The company flourished. Jenny and Peter were able to expand phenomenally and, interestingly, even the most reputable of their customers did not enquire too closely into the unusually favourable terms which they were now being offered. More employees were taken on but no one who would be too inquisitive. Even when they needed a bookkeeper Jenny and Peter made sure that they employed someone who was not only ignorant of accountancy but someone, also, who had good reason to keep his head down.

One of the people upstairs, a boy who was going through a sex-change and was actually working as a woman prostitute called Diana, had a boyfriend called Michael who had just come out of the Merchant Navy. I remember that one day Diana came down and said, 'Can't you find him a job? I can't have him up there while the punters are there.' 'What a good idea.' Michael was not inquisitive, he appreciated the need to keep your own counsel as do most people who live on the wrong side of the law. The laws against poncing ensured that he had something to hide. Even though his relationship with Diana was a good one he could still be charged with 'living off immoral earnings' — so having a job would put him in the clear if Diana were to be arrested. He was also a very social person and would always be ready for the pub at opening hours! Poking his nose around the office would definitely not be his style.

The Company moved to much bigger premises, took on even more staff and arranged security, in the form of a telephonist and other staff, so that Jenny and Peter would never be surprised by unexpected visitors. The 'state' of the franking-meter's register was constantly in their minds and they calculated the amounts on register which would give either maximum or minimum plausibility to the various stories which they might put forward if they were ever caught.

We would always be aware of the franking-meter, where it was and what stage it was at. We knew that if we were ever caught for the full amount that it would mean a long prison sentence. Yet most of the time we felt confident and often used it at the maximum, because otherwise we had to spend twelve hours getting it to run through to the noughts in order to present it at the Post Office. Then, for a short time, they changed the model and put fewer numbers in the ascending register and during that period we only had to spend one hour on every occasion that we wanted to present it to the Post Office. When they changed the model yet again and we were back to twelve hours at a time we felt both very resentful and very nervous about it. It had to be run through for twelve hours during the night when we were least likely to be disturbed. But even then we were nervous. The machine could easily be heard, it was an unusual activity, and anyone could come up to the office and wonder what was going on. So we hired a garage, soundproofed it and from then on, when we had to do a long run, we took the franking-meter there and ran it through in the middle of the night.

Jenny and Peter began to reap the rewards of their white-collar crime and, as with most business crimes, those rewards were consistently and phenomenally high as compared with the usually meagre or one-off earnings picked up from 'non-business' crimes against property. Jenny bought a house in Brighton for herself and one for her mother in Dulwich. Peter bought a house in Tangiers and Jenny was able to enjoy holidays there and elsewhere abroad, though she still kept on her rented flat in Central London. By the end of the 1960s The Company had moved to larger premises in Waterloo and they were now at the peak of their success. But Jenny was becoming bored.

Gender Business

As is often the case with careerist professionals and ambitious business people, Jenny, at the pinnacle of her business career, began to realize that she had achieved success at the expense of her emotional life. She had realized at an early age both that her preferred sexual orientation was towards women and that this was a sexual orientation which was best kept hidden from the outwardly conventional people of her childhood world. But there had been no problem for Jenny herself about this, she had kept her own counsel about her sexual activities and if others would have disapproved, if they had known, then too bad — that would have been their problem, not hers. She had scarcely left school when she had begun the idyllic and hedonistic life with Marie, and that life had satisfied all her needs — emotional, mental and psychological. It was only after she had broken up with Marie that the 'splitting' occurred.

In the mid-1960s there was no easily visible and popular women's movement which could hearten those women who, though non-political in conventional terms, were rejecting the conventional and dominant modes of sexuality and womanhood. Worse, for women like Jenny who wanted to fashion their own lives, conventional modes of sexuality could also include conventional modes of homosexuality.

> When I'd first come to London with the Johnnie Ray crew I'd tripped off to see what the lesbian clubs had on offer and I was appalled! Women passing for men! Stereotyped pairs with pints of beer and gin-and-tonics, carbon copies of what I'd always rejected. No thanks.

So when she broke up with Marie, Jenny decided that she would
bide her time before committing herself to another relationship. In
the meantime she would put all her energies into the business. And
there was the irony! Jenny, who had refused to celebrate her
sexual orientation by becoming a surrogate male in her personal
life, had then found that, in order to succeed, she was required to
act like a surrogate male in her business life! But Jenny was very
principled, and had refused to compromise. If she were going to
make it in The Company then she would do it on her own terms . . .
as a woman of her own making.

> From the time I joined The Company, I was out to prove
> something. I was determined to be respected and powerful as
> a woman in a man's world. I soon realized what I was up
> against. People treated Peter with deference; with me they
> were more hesitant. I thought that I was giving out the same
> signals as him — but, of course, I was a woman! They
> questioned my competence, they questioned my authority;
> they didn't question his. I mastered it, but I had to work twice
> as hard as Peter in order to get there. He could afford to let
> up now and again but I couldn't. Everything about me had to
> say, 'I'm the boss.'

Yet what kind of place was there for a woman who rejected the
conventional and approved modes of female sexuality, refused the
conventional and approved female roles and, additionally, refused
to embrace the conventional gender dualism which, under certain
conditions and at a certain price, permits certain females to enact
the part of surrogate males? To fashion a model of womanhood
which violated *all* conventional conceptions of gender was
impossible without the support of, and identification with, other
women engaged in the same enterprise. Jenny had no contact with
anyone who was self-consciously feminist. The inevitable result
was an emotional and mental isolation both from men and women.

> I knew that I was lesbian but this was the sixties and it was
> still difficult to meet anyone. I'd always been secretive about
> my sex life and I did not want to take on the battle of coming

out if it would interfere with my plans to become a successful businesswoman. At the intellectual level I found most women silly. They irritated me with their stoical acceptance of their second-class status. I had got out, why couldn't they? My attitude to the poor homeworkers was similar, especially towards the enclosers whom I saw as a real underclass; if I could make it, why couldn't they? The only two good things about prison was that it taught me to reject capitalist values and it turned me into a feminist. That hadn't been the Home Office's plan, of course!

But all that was to be in the future. In 1969 Jenny and Peter were exulting in a wealth that enabled Peter to own an aeroplane and a club in Tangiers and Jenny to begin to think about the attractions of leaving The Company and buying some straight businesses. Her continuing thirst for excitement, however, was to take her in a different direction.

Routine Business

The ethics of the franking-machine fraud did not worry Jenny. She found it easy to justify it to herself.

It never disgusted me, it never upset my own morality. I knew it was a crime and I was aware of the possible consequences, but I never felt that it was wrong morally. It was the only logical thing we could have done, to make that business successful and profitable. No one knew about it so I didn't have to justify it to anyone else. We lived a totally double life, and outwardly we were very respectable. We were providing jobs and absolutely no one suspected what we were up to.

It was not the hypocrisy of the double life which upset Jenny, it was the strain of it which troubled her. She, who had striven so hard to be independent of others' definitions now, ironically, had to dissemble in every area of her life — except when she was with Peter. The running of the business, meanwhile, had become so routine that they had become complacent enough to allow someone else to do the franking.

We at last employed someone to do the franking — Edward, a man from Mauritius who could not speak a word of English. Like Michael, the bookkeeper, this man was ideal for our purposes. He was a very nervous man and so timid! We trained him never to allow anyone into the room to look at the franking-meter. (After all it was our Dorian Gray, it literally bore the marks of all our crimes!) And we built up so much suspicion between this Mauritian and the rest of the staff that they did not like him and were glad to keep out of his way. As for us, the management of the crime was so boring that after a few years we were having as little to do with it as possible. By 1972 my one aim was to make as much quick money as I could and then get out. After all, by then I had been at it for some eight years. I think that it was my boredom that led to the beginning of our downfall.

One day someone came into our office, threw a cheque for six-thousand pounds on the table and said, 'Do you want that?' He was running what was quite a well-known fraud at the time. He sent out invoices which, at first sight, looked like *demands* for payment and which inefficient Accounts Offices would pay up without ever looking at the small print which would say 'This is not a demand for payment.' I told Peter that I definitely wanted to do it and he said 'Well, do it, if you want to; you've never asked me before about anything.' So we did it. Now I think that this must have been the beginning of the end. This man had done this fraud all over the world and he was canny. He knew that there would be inquiries from Scotland Yard, he knew that the Board of Trade would come in. So he himself had a very tiny office, kept absolutely no records there and gave them absolutely no information at all when they went to see him. It was then, I think, that they must have begun to examine his mailing. Examination of his envelopes would, of course, have eventually led them to our franking-machine. But around this time we were getting very careless and lazy anyhow and we might have given ourselves away on more than one occasion. For instance, Peter had fallen foul of a couple of chaps from the Post Office . . . *perhaps* they got suspicious, I don't know. I remember that one of them once came in when I was being so lazy and careless that I'd brought the machine up to the office and was running it through there . . . *maybe* it was that, I don't know. Around that time too I was getting more interested in things outside The Company, and for the first time in my life I had started to mix with people who were outwardly criminals — and it was a relief.

One of Peter's clubs was a male homosexual club in the West End. It was there that I met someone who, in reply to my conventional 'And what do you do?' said, 'I'm a thief.' It was such a relief to meet someone who could come straight out with it like that. I was still the 'goody', the upright businesswoman, but I was surrounding myself with people who admitted to committing frauds, bank robberies etc. It was exciting and it was a relief to know that these people, even though they didn't know what Peter and I were doing, wouldn't have cared if they had known. Peter disapproved of my mixing with them because he, in common with other white-collar criminals, thought that he was superior to that kind of person. I, meanwhile, was becoming conscious that beneath the surface I was a criminal too, that anyone who distinguished between my crime and other more conventionally criminal activities was guilty of holding a double standard of morality. For two years I enjoyed the glamour, excitement and easy cameraderie of the criminal underworld. Then we were raided.

The Business of The Courts

If we hadn't become so complacent, bored and routine about the whole business, we might have seen the signs that something was beginning to happen. The first sign was an odd one. Every year there was a dinner dance with the Post Office — it was held for their very big customers. Then, in 1972, the Post Office people at our table did not turn up. We thought, 'That's strange.' We even laughed about it and said, 'Perhaps they've found out and can't meet us at this level any more.' But we still shrugged it off. Then, a few weeks later there were signs that someone was watching us. Questions began to be asked, too many questions, but we were not sure what they meant. Then they phoned up and asked us to bring in the meter! At that point the meter was quite near to the end of its run, so Peter went round to finish it off and readjust it. Outside the office there was a mystery man watching us — wearing half glasses and reading the newspaper upside down! He was later to appear as prosecuting witness at the Old Bailey.

We were still confident that, once the machine was in order and back with the Post Office, everything would be alright. But, ridiculously, we had left incriminating stuff lying around the office. We would never have been so careless a few years before. We had become fed up with the business, fed up with each other and should have called it a day long before.

They arrived on the morning after we had returned the machine. Peter wasn't there, I was. They were the Post Office police and the Fraud Squad. Very well-mannered, very polite, they allowed me to phone home. For they had already told me that the police were outside all our homes, waiting to go in. They were even outside our parents' homes. Oddly enough, my first concern was the drugs. I had two-thousand Dexedrin and another couple-of-thousand purple hearts in my wardrobe. (I used to hand them round at parties|as if they were sweets!) It was lucky, therefore, that they allowed me to phone the guy who was sharing the flat. I remember saying, 'I've got some dirty linen in the wardrobe; as I've got the police here and won't be able to get back, will you make sure that the laundry goes off today?' Fortunately he caught on and was able to get rid of the pills before the raid.

I'd never had a conviction up to that time. I knew that I was breaking the law with the drugs and I knew that I had had stolen goods in my flat. But stolen goods never stayed there long, the drugs were removed before the police arrived and the meter was back to normal. So really, at that point in time, I still wasn't too worried.

The police went through everything at the office, then they took me home. They searched everything thoroughly and they found nothing. We were not arrested. This was my out. I told Peter that I was never going to the office again and that I'd make do with the money that I'd already taken out of The Company. At that time I had enough money to buy two sandwich-bars and a night-club.

Jenny bought the sandwich-bars and the night-club, but found now that she had less money and much more time to spend it in. Wanting to maintain the lifestyle to which she had become accustomed, she decided to go into the Trades' Directory business, another borderline business fraud.

Much of advertising is dishonest and the Trades' Directory fraud just takes these dishonest principles to an extreme. It involves sending out 'advertising' in the form of an invoice with the very small print saying 'this is not a demand for payment' while all the rest of the form bears injunctions to 'pay'. A proportion of these misleading advertisements were always taken to be invoices and paid without question by inefficient Accounts Departments. At the time I did it this particular con was not illegal and was still only an offence against 'Fair Trading'.

I was still living in Sussex Gardens, still very happy with my life. Then, one year after the police raid, I had a phone-call from the police. It was terse and to the point: 'We now have a case and we will be charging you. We want you to come in and answer your case. Find yourselves two sureties of seven-thousand five-hundred pounds each to stand bail for you' ... and we will all be very civilized and above-board. That was the gist of it!

I phoned Marie, whom I had kept in touch with all these years and she was staggered. I phoned Mother Lena and she just couldn't understand. She said, 'I always knew there was something about that Peter. It's tax, isn't it?' I never even explained either to her or to Marie. I just said baldly that I was in trouble. We went into Bow Street Police-Station and it was still all very civilized. We were charged with conspiring to defraud the Post Office and told that we would have to wait about a year before the case came to Court. I think that it was then that I realized that I would go to prison.

Jenny decided that she would make the most of the time that was left to her.

THE
NORTHERN COLLEGE
LIBRARY

BARNSLEY

Peter was trying all kinds of things. He was trying to pay off his debts and he was trying to get a good case going. He got me to agree to ask the police if they would drop the conspiracy charge and accept that either one of us did it. But the police refused, they wanted to go for the conspiracy. Then he talked to someone about paying someone off and that didn't work either. For myself I couldn't really have cared one way or the other. I just went to a solicitor, told him my case, saw a barrister and withheld my options.

In the meantime I continued with the Trades' Directory business and eventually I was arrested for that. So my first ever conviction was brought about through the Office of Fair Trading deciding that I had a case to answer in relation to the Directory business. In the last month of that fraud I had earned twenty-two-thousand pounds but I was only fined three-hundred pounds. As things turned out I never even paid that three-hundred pounds; I did time for it concurrently with my prison sentence.

Now that the police were on to us we were never left alone. My flat was raided by the Chelsea police and they planted marihuana. So my second conviction was for allowing my house to be used for smoking marihuana. That particular conviction was important because from then on they could raid my house any time they liked. They did similar things to Peter — raided his Club and did him for after-hours drinking and so on.

All this time I was still leading an exciting life, drinking, taking drugs, chartering planes to go to Scotland for the weekend, spending a tremendous amount of money. My Directory business had been legal to start with, then they had changed the law, got it wrong and had had to amend it again by Act of Parliament! It was not the first time that a change in the law had instantly criminalized me, but this time I knew enough to enjoy being one step ahead of them. Of course it was a con but I saw it as a challenge to my business expertise. I enjoyed navigating my way around the law.

The turnabout came when I attempted to go on holiday to Italy. When we got to Dover our car was searched, someone found out that I was on bail and that was it. They thought that I was running away and they advised Marie that it would be in my own interest if she withdrew the surety. (This is an emotional ploy which the police frequently use with the friends and relatives of someone whose bail they wish to get withdrawn.)

At the court in Dover I didn't trust the solicitor to speak for me. I put forward my own story and I must say that the woman magistrate listened very carefully and didn't send me to Holloway, which was what the prosecution was asking for. I found another person to stand bail for me but from then on I had to sign on at the police station once a week. Then I did begin to feel much more like a criminal. I had to mix with others who were signing their bail and it was a bit degrading. The net was closing in on me. The bank charged me with fraud on an account which had been kept overdrawn for years. I now really had to start wheeling and dealing, raising money on my property and so on. Also, with the fraud case coming nearer I had to start seriously considering my defence.

The day came when the case went for trial at the Old Bailey. In the dock were Peter, me, Michael the bookkeeper and Edward the man who had done the franking. Neither Michael nor Edward had ever known what was going on. That had been the whole point of employing two people who would never be inquisitive.

My defence was that I had done it on my own. As the police had managed to collect more evidence against me than against Peter it was reasonable to suppose that such a defence might work. If they had accepted that defence then we would all have gone free because we had only been charged with the conspiracy — no separate charges of fraud. So I didn't go into the witness box. I just spoke from the dock and it was like a performance. The case went on for a long time and it was such a complex case that I'm sure that the jury didn't understand most of what went on in Court. At last the judge summed up, the jury went out and it was then, at that point, that my bail was withdrawn and I was kept in custody.

Prison Business

The jury returned after about three hours and we were all found guilty. Peter got five years, Michael twenty-one months and Edward eighteen months suspended. Edward burst into tears; he still hadn't a clue what it was all about. Because my barrister wasn't in Court the judge said that he would sentence me next day as he thought that I should have my barrister in Court to give mitigation.

I went off to Holloway where I shared a cell with a woman with a glass eye. She was in for grievous bodily harm — 'only me husband' — and she told me that she had hit him with an axe! It was amazing how I accepted this woman. I wasn't frightened at all, just numb. Next day when I went back to court, the judge said that I had wielded an evil influence over the whole criminal enterprise and I got five years as well. In retrospect it is interesting to note that Peter wasn't described as evil. Far from it — the male judge described him as a Walter Mitty character! I went downstairs to the cells and I slept. It was such a relief that at last it was all over.

The reception at Holloway was quite horrific. There were women there who had been in police cells for days and had not had a proper wash. There were women at various stages of shock or trauma — some withdrawing from drugs or drink — and all of us had had our clothes taken from us and were wrapped in those horrible towelling dressing-gowns. I was put in this small box like a horse box and I sat there eating the piece of white bread and butter and cold sausage which had been given me. First, I was marched down to a WVS woman who said, 'Can I do anything for you?' I said, quite genuinely, 'Well, what can you do?' and she didn't seem to know, so I said, 'No thanks.' I went back to the horse box. I didn't know how long I was going to wait there. My whole time sequence — all the things which you rely on to structure your life — they just didn't exist any more. Then I was told to have a bath — in about three or four inches of water — and I had to get in and out in front of an officer. Next I was marched off to be examined. I had to stand naked on a bench and jump off —

to see if anything fell out of my vagina, I suppose — and then they looked under my breasts. I was in an awful state because the shock of my sentence had started off my period and although I had asked for a tampax I hadn't been given one.

Last, I was called to the reception counter. The officer said, 'So we've got you for five years. I've just heard about you on the radio. Famous are you? Well, you won't be famous here.' I was then sent off to a unit in Old Holloway.

It was in prison that Jenny began to realize once more the creative and self-renewing possibilities of being a successful woman in a woman's world. For too long she had been striving to present herself as a woman who could successfully compete with businessmen. Her earlier life with Marie had taught her some of the satisfactions of non-competitive creativity. Now, in prison, some of her old values began to resurface.

Women's Business

So there I was in Holloway, living with all these women again, and it was something I hadn't done for many years. I was a bit nervous about who I was going to meet, but the very first thing that struck me was how caring and considerate the other prisoners were. It was a good thing that they were because the officers told you absolutely nothing. For instance, I'd never done anything domestic; I didn't even know how to scrub a floor but a woman who saw me scrubbing for the first time said, 'Come here, and let me show you, you don't do it like that.' Other women told me where you could get sanitary towels and tissues. The friendship on the wing was quite supportive and, because I was with long-term prisoners, I was particularly struck by the amount of laughing and joking which went on. I realized that I could respect these women, that they hadn't been ground down at all.

Between me and the officers there was a big brick wall. I wasn't frightened of them but from the moment I went in I decided that on the one hand they'd never be able to get me for anything and that on the other I'd never be asking them for any favours. My way of coping with my prison sentence was to make friends with the other women. During my time with The Company I had got into the way of treating women as being silly and second class and as a result I had been starved of women's friendship for a long time. (It can happen to married women too, of course, not just to women like me who go into business.) Once I got to prison I began to feel that I had a common bond with the other women. When I had first gone in I had really felt very superior to the women who had done burglaries, GBH, those kinds of crimes. But gradually I began to realize that what many of us had in common was that we had been guilty of allowing men to make our decisions for us. This wasn't entirely true in my own case but from talking to the other women I soon learned that many of them had committed their crimes either for their men or for their children and that very few of them seemed to have got any of the proceeds for themselves. At the end of the day, however, they were the ones in prison and realizing that they now had to take responsibility for themselves. No longer could any of us see ourselves just in relation to men. In prison, therefore, I learned to live my life for me. I learned to become emotionally independent. I didn't become selfish but I freed myself from the guilt that other people had always made me feel about being me. I began to build a new life.

Jenny stayed at Holloway for eight months and as she began, as she puts it, 'to strip away the myths from the reality' she developed a tremendous thirst for knowledge. She began doing English and Maths O levels with a view to eventually taking an Open University degree and, for the first time in her life, she became politically aware of inequality and injustice. Then she was moved to Durham's notorious 'H' wing.

Going to Durham was a shocking experience. In 'H' Wing you are under maximum surveillance, twenty-four hours a day. My own crime and record didn't warrant maximum security but the Home Office sends women there who have been convicted of fairly minor crimes so that they can make up the numbers. So I was sent to Durham neither for my own good nor for the public good, but purely to suit the convenience of the Home Office.

At Durham a prisoner's every movement is monitored and controlled. You have to be very quiet and you can get told off for *laughing*. The regime is totally oppressive. Even when you're locked in your cell someone will look through the Judas-hole every hour, on the hour. There is an electronic lock on the door and once you're locked in you cannot get taken out of your room unless the Governor is called out of his bed. They can't even push a sanitary towel or a pill through to you if you get taken ill. You move about in very small spaces and only three women can talk together at one time — though never behind a closed door. You always have to leave the door open. Tension builds up. I met some interesting women in Durham and I took two Open University courses there but I changed physically, emotionally and mentally. My skin became grey and I looked harder. I began to walk differently — much more aggressively — and I learned to hate.

I remember learning to hate for the first time. One day I looked out through the barred window of my cell and saw male officers marching a man round and round a tiny exercise yard. Watching them were other officers with dogs and chains and batons. At that moment I felt absolute hatred.

I almost became violent too. Once when another prisoner was getting on my nerves I grabbed hold of her by the throat and almost thumped her in the face. I was very shaken by the incident, though I knew that it was a result of all the tension that had built up. I began to withdraw into my own head. I had led a totally different life to Josie (see chapter four), but prison can make even the most stable women withdraw into their own heads. Once the process begins, you start not going down to meals; some people ask to be locked up in solitary, on rule 43; other people keep themselves to themselves. Everyone does it differently but the prison staff are trained to treat you all the same — as prisoners. You stand by helpless, watching your own suffering being mirrored in others.

I had been at Durham for twelve months when one day, completely out of the blue, I was told that I was to be sent to Askham Grange open prison. I was tipped straight out of a concrete tomb into an open prison in the middle of Yorkshire.

At first, Jenny hated Askham Grange. Being locked up in close confinement is totally debilitating and when Jenny first went to Askham she could not even bring herself to plug in the kettle to make a cup of tea. For a year she had not engaged in routine domestic activities; for a year, her every move had been monitored; now that she was released into open conditions she could not cope with them! But although the Askham regime was more relaxed in some ways it was stricter in others. Spatially, the women were less confined but, because of the very high standards of behaviour required of them, they were even more closely regulated both physically and mentally. Hundreds of petty rules, violation of any of them possibly resulting in loss of pay and privileges, ensured that the women never forgot that they were in prison.

> I hated the pettiness of it all, the kind of things you were put on report for. I'd managed to get that far without getting a report but at Askham I lost two weeks' pay just for picking a handful of blackberries. Someone else lost two days' remission for having a piece of bread in her room. You could be put on report for running up the stairs.

Jenny never lost her contempt for the pettiness of Askham's disciplinary regime but, once she had settled in, she began to piece together the different bits of her new feminist and political perspectives. From these new perspectives she reviewed her life so far and decided that in future she would break free of the coercive role demands of others, that, in future, she would write the scripts herself.

> I had already become politicized through the Open University and now the feminist influences were getting to me. Together with some other prisoners, exciting and independent women bursting with creativity and enthusiasm for life, I became a founder member of what is now the women ex-prisoners' theatre company, Clean Break. We decided to do plays written for women by women and, fortunately, we were lucky enough to have the support and encouragement of the woman Governor and a feminist teacher. The majority of officers, however, were very much against us working in this way. Clean Break was seen as being anarchic; women actually

having fun, making decisions for themselves and doing something positive with their prison experience.

And that's exactly what Clean Break is for me . . . women together taking responsibility for their actions, breaking the bonds of class, race and gender and enjoying their lives to the full.

Postscript: Coming Out

I was released in March 1979. My capitalist-inspired dreams were forgotten. In their place I had two not quite congruent feelings: an anger born of all the miseries, inequalities and injustices which I had learned about in prison; and an optimism born of the collective talents and energies released by Clean Break. As I walked out of Askham Grange I knew that although my real world was still 'inside' I had, somehow, to make this now alien 'outside' world a reality once more. I had already accepted the offer of accommodation and a job in a florists from two friends from the past and in this, as in the continuing support and love of my two mothers, I was exceptionally fortunate. The majority of newly-released women do not have a home, job and family to come out to. Yet, despite my good fortune, my education and my will to continue with the creative reconstruction of my life along feminist and socialist lines, my life as an ex-prisoner has been one long obstacle race past prejudice, suspicion, bureaucratic indifference and condescension — often from those very organizations whose whole *raison d'être* is supposed to be rooted in ex-prisoners' welfare. I stayed a short time at the florist's and then did a three-year course at Rose Bruford College. I received no grant for the first year of my college course, although I could have had a grant if I had accepted the Central School of Speech and Drama's offer of a place on a more conservative course. But I wanted to keep true to my new principle of doing what I considered was right for me. So, rather than putting financial considerations first, I went to Rose Bruford and funded myself by doing part-time jobs. It was not easy to struggle through and there were times when I wondered if it was worth the effort. I was tempted to go back to business with all the fraudulent practices which that would involve. The thought of prison was certainly no deterrent to me; once you've been to prison it is no longer 'the bogey' and, furthermore, the debilitating effects of imprisonment combined with the prejudice and continuing 'punishment' of ex-prisoners can even make one feel pushed back towards prison. Nor had imprisonment in itself made me a better person. Anything for good that had happened to me had been effected despite the system. People will say that there are some good and caring people in the penal system. That is true, but they are the exception rather than the rule and the system does not reward them for their efforts. The education officer at Holloway Prison was an exception in the system, and I was lucky to meet him. The Governor of Askham Grange was an exception, and we were fortunate to have her support for Clean Break. But both of these officials were opposed by the majority of prison officers and by other officials. So it was not the prison, but the Women's Movement, which was important in my development. The prison experience is so extreme, degrading, humiliating and isolating that prisoners' initial sense of guilt and shame at their crime is soon replaced by feelings of injustice and alienation from the society which can treat them so. It is for this reason that ex-prisoners need to help each other. Clean Break is successful because we are self-organized. So much money is spent on funding various agencies set up for prisoners but these are rarely successful because ex-prisoners treat them with suspicion and generally avoid them. In 1981 an ex-prisoner from Holloway set up another ex-prisoner-organized project. With the help of the education department at Holloway she formed The Creative and Supportive Trust (known as CAST), a centre to give space, facilities and support to women who want to develop creative talents which will, eventually, enable them to become financially self-supporting — though always the emphasis is upon women's need for intrinsic satisfaction rather than upon the pursuit of profit. However, through lack of adequate funds, prisoner-run groups like Clean Break and CAST are always working on a shoe-string — as when, for instance, Clean Break played one time in Liverpool and the whole cast lived off the proverbial bag of chips! In 1983 I joined the campaigning group Women In Prison (see p. 187) and in

January 1984 I was offered a part-time paid post with WIP. In February 1984 I was offered another part-time post — this time with CAST to work with Clean Break Theatre Company from the CAST base. After a long struggle I was at last being paid a full-time salary for doing work that I wanted to do — and had indeed already been doing for a long time for no pay! So I have achieved some success in my new life — but it has been incredibly difficult. Without Clean Break and the help of other ex-prisoners I would not have made it. Women who come out of prison desperately need help to repair the damage which prison does, but the help they need is of a material and non-paternalistic kind; the financial and other material backing which can enable them to organize a variety of projects within which they can best maintain the autonomy and independence which they value. On the basis of my own experience, therefore, I am convinced that self-organization is the only way forward for women who want to find a satisfying alternative to crime.

4

Josie: Surviving Holloway . . . and other Women's Prisons

Josie O'Dwyer and Pat Carlen

Britain has six closed prisons for women: Holloway in London, Styal in Cheshire, Cookham Wood in Kent, a wing of Durham prison, Cornton Vale just outside Stirling in Scotland and Armagh Prison in Northern Ireland.

For England and Wales there is one closed Youth Custody Centre, Bullwood Hall in Essex and an open Youth Custody Centre, at East Sutton Park. There are three open prisons for women: Drake Hall in Staffordshire, Askham Grange in Yorkshire and East Sutton Park in Kent. The three remand centres which take women and girls are: Low Newton in Durham, Pucklechurch in Bristol and Risley in Cheshire. Scotland has no open prison for women as all penal facilities — remand wing, young prisoners' wing, Youth Custody Centre and prison — are concentrated on one site at Her Majesty's Institution, Cornton Vale. In Northern Ireland a separate part of Armagh Prison is used as the female young offenders' centre. Additionally, women on remand are often held for one night (or more) in police-cells and, at various times, certain convicted women prisoners have been temporarily housed in one of the male institutions. Josie O'Dwyer has served sentences (or been remanded) at Pucklechurch, Bullwood Hall, Cookham Wood, Styal, Holloway and Mountjoy Gaol in Ireland. Although she is only twenty-eight she has, since the age of fourteen, spent eight of those twenty-eight years in a variety of penal institutions, including Approved School, Borstal, Remand Centre, and four closed prisons. And Josie has survived. The purpose of this chapter, therefore, is to describe exactly how Josie did survive those years and, in telling the story of one prisoner's survival, to describe also

138

the violence, the injustices, the pain, the degradations and the other, different modes of survival (or not) which characterize British women's imprisonment.

Surviving Care

On any day of the year around fifteen hundred women are held captive in British prisons. Many of them will be remand prisoners, only twenty-seven per cent of whom will eventually receive a custodial sentence; over a quarter of the convicted women will be in prison for failing to pay a fine, and over half of them will be there for some minor crime of stealing. Of the remainder, less than ten per cent of the convicted women will have been found guilty of violent crime and a sizeable number of prisoners in all categories will be those whose biographies embody accounts of all kinds of social, emotional and mental problems often either unrelated or related only tangentially to their criminal activities. A sizeable number of this latter group, too, will have either been brought up in institutions from an early age or will have been taken into either 'Care' or the old Approved-School System in their early teens. Either way these 'state-raised' children will have learned early on in their careers that the main name of the game in institutions is SURVIVAL.

Josie O'Dwyer is just one of the many women whose penal careers began at the age of fourteen in circumstances which make a mockery of the terms 'care', 'training' and 'in the child's best interest'.[1] Josie's account of her first taste of the penal system is one which, like many other accounts (see Diana Christina's in chapter two and Jimmy Boyle's[2]) is studded with references to feelings of fear and memories of violence. As a consequence of being apprehended by the police for 'breaking and entering' the full force of the penal and judicial machinery engulfed the adolescent Josie in a quick processing through police-cell, prison remand-wing and Approved School.

> They took me in a police-car, up the motorway to Bristol. I was only little: aged fourteen, four-feet-ten inches in height and just six stone. It seemed a long journey from Exeter to Bristol and I was terrified, absolutely terrified. But I was stroppy with it. I had already spent the night in the police-cell

at Exeter and I had been in a cell with a junkie who was really sick. I got myself in the top bunk and sat in the corner clutching a pillow; I actually chewed off the corner of that pillow watching this woman thrashing about. Then in the morning they took me to Pucklechurch. They had told me that it was a remand centre but it looked like a prison. I had thought that it was going to be a kids' home, maybe with bars on the windows so that I couldn't get out, but it wasn't, it was a real prison. They took me to the women's section and the police handed me over to the prison officers. All that I wanted to do was to curl up in a corner with something over my head and stay there, but I had to get undressed. I took my clothes off and put on this dressing-gown and I felt terrified. I've never felt such fear and yet the prison officers were being really nice to me compared with how I've seen them since with other people! They eventually coaxed me out with cigarettes and took me down this long corridor with cell doors on either side. They took me to a cell, locked me up for the night and came along in the morning and said that I was to go and see the Chief. I wouldn't get dressed though. I was still terrified, still had the dressing-gown over my head. Then I looked out of the window and I saw the prisoners exercising in the yard. I couldn't believe my eyes; I really thought that some of them were men! The prison officers kept coming in and encouraging me to go out and exercise — 'Come on, love' etc., but I would not go.

Josie was terrified and, as is often the case when people are afraid, she soon realized that one effective way to counter one's own fear is to inspire fear in others. Women's prisons, no less than men's, are places of violence; places where explicit violence will gain credit for its perpetrators and where a known capacity for violence is the necessary currency for efficient and healthy survival. In prison, moreover, the newcomer does not have to be pre-disposed to violence in order to engage in violent modes of behaviour — lessons in violence come at her from all sides.

In the cell next to me there was a Pakistani woman; I think that she was waiting to be deported. They had taken her baby away from her because she had kept trying to kill herself and the baby. She actually wrecked her cell, there was a lot of blood and I was terrified. Then I wrecked my own cell. I put all the windows out and smashed all the furniture. The officers came in and told me to take all my clothes off. Then they put me in this special dress and did something up at the neck so that it could not be taken off. It took me four hours to chew through it. I wouldn't come out of that cell for ten days and then I came out to go to church. After that the prison officers managed to coax me out for the last hour of Association and I was amazed at everyone wanting to mother me because I was so tiny. They gave me chocolates and they wanted me to sit on their lap. I didn't mind at all, I liked it. Then came the bombshell. I was told that I was being moved to the Approved School.

Within the penal system those who want to survive counter their own fear by inspiring fear in others and meet violence with violence or, better still, the threat of violence. Boredom and loss of freedom, however, call for different survival tactics and in the case of children and young people held in less secure conditions, the most obvious way to regain their freedom and self-respect is to go straight back out, either over the wall or through the gate. Josie was eventually to find that, in fact, the senior Approved School provided a good academic education but when she first arrived there was no way that she intended to stay. She became a 'runner'.

Seventeen times I ran away from that school and seventeen times they took me back. Each time they took me back I spent twenty-four hours in the detention room. I eventually dislocated my knee jumping out of a window but I still tried to run away, on crutches! Next morning they gave me a skirt to put on, but I kept my jeans on and went for the nearest window, with tennis-rackets and anything else that came to hand. The school was in Bath and I used to run back to Truro. I don't know what I was running to really; it was just an instinct. If I could get out, I got out.

But Josie, recognizing that she, like many other runners, had in reality no one and nowhere to run to, eventually settled down to

O levels, horse-riding, forced religion (it was a Convent school) and more lessons in the seamier side of life.

> There were girls who had been through more than me, they had been prostitutes. It was mostly sex they talked about and sex was seen as a crime anyway, because we were in a Convent school. Some of those girls went on to remand centres and then to Borstal.

When Josie left the school at sixteen the process of her social isolation and stigmatization as a delinquent had already begun.

> I was sixteen when I left. I had never had a letter or a visit all the time that I had been there. I went back to Cornwall and tried for various jobs but they soon found out about my past, what I'd done and where I'd been, and they weren't prepared to forgive and forget. I used to sit for hours and stare into space. None of my friends understood; they all thought that I was mad. After about five months I took myself back up to Bath and it was there that I overdosed — I just didn't know what to do next. Then I actually went breaking and entering with the full intention of getting myself nicked.

Surviving Borstal[3]

> I went to Borstal after I had been convicted on a burglary charge. They sent me off to Bullwood Hall along with two others and again, I was terrified. This time there was real reason to be afraid. An air of viciousness pervaded the whole place. The tougher you were the better. If you weren't tough people insulted you and took your cigarettes off you. You had a dog's life. It's the way the prison officers ran it which made it like that. Inmates couldn't really retaliate, but having a go at an officer gave them some kind of credit. They tore up each other's photos and ripped up each other's clothes. I'd been on the Assessment Unit for about five days and it was my first night on the wing when I happened to be going for a bath that I saw one inmate being kicked by about five others. It was not done quickly to get it over with; they were actually thoroughly enjoying it. The message was 'Don't mix-it with

us.' Everyone was frightened of everybody else. Anything could start off a fight. Everything or nothing. The officers could have stopped it if they'd wanted to. They could have run the place differently. They stood down on the ground floor and everything that went on that was bad went on either on the landings or in somebody's cell — and in the recess anyhow. Unless you were one of the toughest you were absolutely terrorized. Borstal was amazing. Whereas the grown women in Pucklechurch could take things in their stride, in Borstal the slightest little thing could make someone hit the ceiling and the officers would just go in. There would be no 'Come on, dear, calm down.' None of that. They just went in and grabbed you and took you off down to the punishment block. You got the same treatment whatever you did so you knew that you might as well hit the roof, make a big show out of it and get some credit out of it.

At that stage Josie did not have time to think about the whys and whereforee of the viciousness which permeated Bullwood. She did not realize then that the viciousness was a product of the system itself rather than of the system's victims. She only had time to suss out how best to ensure her own survival.

You weren't allowed to do your sentence quietly. You survived by being the most vicious. But you couldn't just be vicious — you also had to have no fear, to be able to take the punishment and the lock-up. At first I was probably the most frightened. I was terrified. The whole place terrified me. The air was electric, always someone doing something, alarm bells going, a fight going on, screaming, shouting, banging. They used to sing 'A . . . G . . . G . . . R . . . O . . .' It was terrible — just bang, bang; bang, bang, bang. You *had* to scream, you had to let go. You just couldn't contain it within yourself. Every single day there was some sort of trouble and people were screaming out of the windows all the time in Bullwood. If one person started banging on the door the whole wing would take it up. I discovered that if I got all wound up, ready to blow, the whole wing would be all simmering, waiting for the action and it gave me credit. But it didn't just come from me, it was there all the time, just waiting for someone to set light to it. You had to have fights with the screws as they dragged you off to punishment because you were considered a cissy if you just walked there. Everyone struggled. They bent your arms so you tried to bite and you spat and kicked. They weren't exactly gentle either. Some of the officers were a little more vicious than the others so you worked out which ones to go for. You worked out who was soft, who was hard and who would hurt you most. So when you saw them coming at you — about eight or nine prison officers and a couple of men in the background — you tried to let the gentler ones get hold of you. To me it was just a game and you had to play the game well or you got hurt. Most of my stuff looked good, but it was all bravado, all for show, to give me more credit, so that I could survive. I never really hurt anyone.

'Smashing-up' is such a feature of younger women's imprisonment that the authorities, rather than admitting to it and investigating it, treat it as an inevitable fact of Borstal 'life'.

Once I smashed the wing to pieces — sink, bath, I wrecked the whole thing. The others were all locked up while the repairs were done but they never said anything about it afterwards. Nobody ever asked why I did the smashing-up. You went in front of the Governor, you didn't cry on your punishment, you never gave anyone's name. You could have black eyes, a split lip, the works, but when the Governor asked what happened you'd say, 'I fell over, Miss.' And she'd just say, 'Behind the door till further notice,' and then you'd get more credit still be creating havoc down in the punishment block. You'd be thinking, 'This is it, now. This is the most they can give me.' No one ever discussed your behaviour. It was as if they didn't care. Once, after I had put a swill bin over an officer's head the Governor came down to punishment and said, 'What can I do to keep my officers on duty when you're about?' 'You'd better get me a fucking punch-ball.' And when I went up to my cell about a week later there was this huge cardboard box with a punch-ball in it and I used to hammer away at it for hours and hours.

On this occasion Josie had been lucky. Most women in the penal system have absolutely no physical outlets for their pent-up emotions. Gymnasia in women's prisons are seldom used and opportunities for games and other physical exercise, such as dancing, are almost nil. Josie's description of her later experience of the (non-)use of the gym at Holloway Prison has been echoed by several other ex-prisoners to whom we have spoken.

> There is a gym but you can only go *when* there is an officer to take you, *when* the gym officer is in and *when* they ask you. Sometimes at Holloway they will ring up and say 'Anyone for gym?' and the landing officer will say, 'No', when she hasn't even asked.

In women's prisons, even the lighting of cigarettes can be a contentious issue — and ten years ago the Bullwood regime was like several other women's regimes in not allowing the women to have lighters for their cigarettes.

> You were allowed cigarettes but you were not allowed matches or lighters. You had to get a light from the pilot-light which was on the landing and you could tell all the new girls because they all had blisters on the ends of their noses.

Not only are the young women tense and frustrated at being *cooped-up* and without exercise they are also *wound-up* in a variety of ways. Sometimes it is their enforced witnessing of the many scenes of bullying and injustice which winds them up. At other times, before they have learned to cope with the wiles of state employees who should know better, they are deliberately wound-up by prison officers who act less like responsible beings and more like super-cats playing with clockwork mice. Women like Josie, already tense with the pains of their own imprisonment, are caught on the raw edge of their emotions when they see prison officers playing on the nerves of those other prisoners who, being the least robust physically, mentally and emotionally, are also those who are least likely to fight back.

> The lower down you were, the worse it was — you copped it from everyone. It was because of that that I was the cause of

the 1973 riots — I actually started them all off. The officers
helped to wind me up.

There was this girl having a visit from her foster Mum. She
was one of those girls right down at the bottom and I think
that she was most likely a bit mentally retarded too. Her
Mum had given her a comic. She had read it about six times
but she wanted to keep hold of it because her Mum had given
it to her. A screw then came along and said, 'Where did you
get that from?' 'My Mum', she said. The screw said, 'You
know you're not supposed to take things from visitors' and
she took the comic off her. Me and some others went and
grabbed the comic back and I said, 'You wouldn't fucking do
that if it was me, would you?' (It was just about this time that I
was realizing that they were treating me differently because
of the come-back.) The officer then backed away, and Lianna
started poking her and saying 'And you wouldn't do it to me,
either, would you?' You could see that she was frightened
and she began to back away into the office and then she
bolted and locked the door.

It was the worst thing she could have done. We started
kicking and banging the door, bust the lock and by this time
the whole wing knew it. We actually made her run the
gauntlet, kicking her. House One joined in and we wrecked
the whole place. The TV, the piano, through the double
doors, down the stairs; it was like a fever. They called in
busloads of prison officers from various places. We had made
barricades of tables. Then the Governor came down to the
wing. I went to speak to the Governor with one inmate either
side of me just as she had two officers one either side of her.
'If you tell the inmates to go down to their cells,' she said,
'they will only stay in there until the repairs are done.' I went,
'Yeh, alright'. So I went back. We all put our arms round
each other's shoulders and our heads together — it was
ridiculous! To them it was all so serious, to us such a game,
just a game we were playing. So I said, 'Look, any chicken
who wants to go back in there can go back, so *she* says: but
it's up to you. It's not going to make any bleeding difference,
cos what's been done's been done.' And I said, 'So what is the
answer?' They just picked up all the plates piled up on the
tables and — shshshrup, smash; over they went! In the end

there was nothing left to throw and they just came and tore us apart. I got beaten quite badly for that, but still I got credit. It's a crazy situation. Most of the girls in Borstal wouldn't do half the things they do in there if they didn't get caught up in that feeling. It just spreads, the whole Borstal is always waiting for something to start. It's an amazing feeling. Young girls in the Borstal for the first time see how the prison officers respond to those who smash-up and they want to be like that too. Because they see that if the prison officers can shit on you and get away with it, then they will. But you have got to take an awful lot of stick in order to *stop* them shitting on you.

By the time Josie had finished her Borstal sentence she had completed her apprenticeship in violence and she was ready for bigger things. She knew that her Borstal days were over and, like many of the other Borstal girls, she knew also that the next stop would be prison.

Most of the girls had an idea that they were going on to prison anyway so you thought that whatever crimes you did when you were out, next time you went in you'd have more 'cred.' It was happening to me like that, though I didn't realize it at the time. But now when I go back and think, I think, 'Huh! What a wally!' Because when I came out of Borstal my ambition in life was to be the top dog, the most hardened criminal, the worst, the most vicious. There was no other reason to be alive as far as I was concerned. Anything outside wasn't going to give me a chance anyway, so if I was going to make it anywhere, it had to be in there.

Surviving Holloway

At both Pucklechurch and Bullwood Hall Josie had viewed her own violent behaviour as being nothing more than part of the general prison game; a game whose rules had already been decided by others; a game which she had usually won. Holloway was to be different. Josie had only been there ten minutes when she battered down the door of her cell. The response was one which she will never forget.

I was seventeen-years old and that was my first taste of brutality. First, there were women officers and then the men came along to take me off to the annexe. There were no women about after that. When the men got hold of me I was in agony. I went the whole way to the annexe — which is quite a distance — with my arms literally twisted up and my feet hardly touching the ground. They got my legs and then my arm so that it was behind the back of my knee with my foot pressed down on top of it, which was very painful. Somebody else got hold of my toes and were pulling them apart. When they do that it's like electricity and you can feel each toe separately. You have to separate your mind from your body all the time and in the dead centre of your head there is something saying, 'They're hurting me on purpose.' This was the horror. I was not even struggling any more, but they were still meaning to hurt me, like torture. They took me down the annexe stairs which are really, really steep and, instead of my feet touching the top bit of the stairs, I went actually touching the inside bits. At the bottom they let me go and I just skidded along on my chin and took all the skin off. I was dragged by my hair into a cell and then my clothes were literally ripped off me. When I was absolutely naked they just kicked me round and round that cell until I curled up and cried like a baby, absolutely naked, in the corner. That was the first real pasting I had.

It was not to be the last. As well as the male officers whose special duty it was to carry obstreperous prisoners off to the strips there were those female officers, the 'heavy mob', who also liked to specialize in violence.

You had the heavy mob, you always had the heavy mob and they were the most vicious and the most frightening of the lot. Some of them would be absolutely massive. When they came for you it was terrifying. Something would happen on the wing and while the officers there would be telling you, 'It's OK calm down etc.' they would be rounding up the heavy mob in the rest of the prison. They accumulated just off the wing, no one at first would actually see them waiting for each other to turn up, and then it would be, nudge, nudge, 'She's had her chance now, here comes the heavy mob'.

When they give you a fucking good hiding they do get their jollies out of it and you can feel that they do. As they are carrying you to the block they are all reaching out for their pound of flesh — pinching you under the arm or on the inside of the thigh. One particular officer always steamed in and started poking you in the chest because she wanted you to hit her — that's what she got off on, the struggling and the fighting. They carry you by the 'necklace', the key chains and you can have three chains round your neck at any one time. You get purple bruises round your neck, a necklace of purple . . . you begin to blackout and you think, 'This is it, I'm going to die now.' I myself 'died' many times in prison because many's the time I've actually passed out going to the block. OK, I was fighting but there were always enough of them to restrain me, for God's sake. There was no need for them to nearly choke me to death. You fall into that blackness at last, and think, 'That's it, I'm dying,' That's your last thought before you wake up and they are stripping you, or you're alone in the cell. Sometimes, if you are still fighting when they get you to the cell they will inject you. If you know that the last time they injected you it didn't work and that *they* know that, then you wonder, 'Are they going to double that fucking dose this time? Will I actually overdose and not wake up again?' After all, you hear about people dying in prison, and no one questioning it.[4] So you say to yourself 'I've spent eight years in some institution or other, I could so easily be put down, and the whole thing could be covered up by them saying: "She was being restrained . . . she was institutionalized . . . it was inevitable"'.

Your life is in their hands, and I could have died. But I didn't and I was lucky. I was a survivor.

The ever-present threats to both physical and psychological survival are accompanied by omnipresent fears of death, physical injury, emotional and psychological damage and madness. At the end of the disciplinary road lies Broadmoor, final lock-up for those young women who dare to take on the system and lose. Yet even though this latter group are in a minority, the *threat* of Broadmoor is at the back of the minds of many prisoners, particularly of those prisoners who realize, at the same time as they are fighting back, that they are also concomitantly damaging themselves. For although officer violence poses one of the main threats to survival in the women's closed prisons, it is not the only one. Other threats to survival include psychiatry, drugs, isolation, provocation ('winding-up' and 'setting-up') by the prison officers, institutionalization and sheer boredom. Survival strategies in their turn are equally, if not more, inventive and varied and we shall be looking at many of them in the course of this chapter. Immediately, however, we wish to describe and discuss the related phenomena of 'winding-up' and 'setting-up', the two major ways in which prison officers can manipulate either the younger or the less stable prisoners so that in becoming emotionally disturbed to the point of violence they are more than ever vulnerable to, and officially deserving of, the prison's more draconian disciplinary techniques. To understand *why* some prisoners can so easily be 'wound-up' and/or 'set-up' by prison officers, it is necessary to remember first, that many women in prison have no one on the outside to care or even wonder about their fate in prison and second, that those women who *do* have families and friends outside are, through prison censorship of letters and prison officer control of visits, cut off from all direct contact with them. As a result, whereas some women are vulnerable to prison officer abuse *because* they have no family, other women's dearest and closest relationships are invoked by prison officers in the service of one of their more exquisite forms of torture — the engendering of fears about a husband's or lover's faithfulness or about a beloved child's safety.

'**Winding-up**' begins as soon as the prisoner arrives at reception and, if the prisoner flips at that stage, prison life from then on can be one big wind-up.

Prisoners can arrive any time from midday right up until nine or ten at night. They have to sit in reception all day. There's three officers in the reception room which is a big glass office. You're told to stand on a towel while these officers go through and mark down each article of clothing. Then they say, 'Right, drop the dressing-gown' and you do a twirl. There's people walking in the corridors while you're doing this. Then they give you your clothes, you have a bath and you go to the Sister who checks for crabs and lice — the whole works. After that you go up and sit in the dining-room waiting to see the doctor for another three or four hours in your dressing-gown. Actually, he doesn't examine you at all so why you have to sit in your dressing-gown all that time is beyond me. He says, 'Are you fit?' You say, 'Yes', and that's it. Then you wait until you've been allocated to the B3s, and the officer comes along with your reception letter and your sheets, and off you go to the B3s where you're put either in a twin-bedded cell or a dormitory.

Nobody tells you what to do, you just follow them. No statutory rule book is issued, nothing. When you're unlocked first thing in the morning you wander out and no one says to you 'You must go up to the dining room and ask them for a place and a knife and fork.' So for the first few days some people don't eat. You're never *told* anything. You have to find out your rights for yourself. For instance, I once had to tell a woman whose family lived in New York that because she couldn't have visits she could have a phone call in lieu.

The indignities of reception, the secrecy of the system, can of themselves wind-up many women. Others are, for a variety of reasons, selected for special treatment by the prison officers themselves.

If they don't like the look of either the prisoner or what she's been charged with, then it's a wind-up job. And prisoners aren't stupid, they know they're being wound-up. You think, 'It must be my turn next', and then the person who came in behind you is called up before you. You think, 'They're trying to wind me up, fucking starting on me already.' Then they'll start making comments about your clothes — your socks smell, didn't you get a wash in the police-cell, things like that, well below the belt. I myself hate coming through reception. I can understand people being wound-up.

One particular inmate I remember. She was only about eighteen, quite cute really, only four foot and a dog-end. She'd been sitting waiting and, because she'd got cold, had put her clothes back on. 'Right', they yelled, 'come on, get your clothes off.' 'You can fucking wait for me now', she said, 'I've been sitting waiting for hours,' and she started shouting. She was unlucky. There were some coffee cups there and she knocked into them and they went over some prison officers. That kid got a pasting. You could see them dragging her up the corridor, taking off their watches . . . of course, they know who to pick on, the kids who've got no one.

The most horrific case I saw when I was working in reception at Holloway was the deaf and dumb woman who came in. She made this noise that actually hit you right in the guts. She didn't understand what was happening and they never bothered booking anyone with sign language. She kept on making the noise and the next thing, she was being dragged up the corridor in a strip dress which rode way above her neck while they were dragging her by the ankles. It was this noise that got me. I actually lost my head, shut both the double doors and shouted, 'I'm fucking reporting you lot.' But there was nothing you could do.

Prisoners do not report officers for fear of being put on a charge of making false and malicious accusations against an officer. Prison officers, on the other hand, having almost complete control of the prisoners' living quarters and timetables, can wind-up prisoners at every moment of the day. Association, visits, letters, prisoners' personal appearances, cell searches — all are but a few of the many potential sites and occasions on which prison officers can wind-up prisoners.

In the old Holloway it was extraordinary *not* to have association but nowadays, in the new Holloway, you can say to an officer at teatime, 'Is there association tonight?' and she'll say, 'Yes', implying that the sooner you get into your cell, the sooner you'll be out. You think, 'Great!' And you sit there waiting for association. I'd be sitting there in my dressing-gown, my stuff ready so that I could be the first in the queue for a bath. Then minutes would go by and I'd think, 'They'll be opening up soon.' Fifteen minutes — not a sound! Then I'd start to think, 'Oh no! . . .' and I'd ring the bell, 'Is there association tonight?' 'No, not tonight.' 'Well, what did you tell me there was association for?' They would just walk away and not answer. By then I'd be really wound-up.

Both of us have heard prison officers reading aloud from prisoners' letters. In Holloway officers use information from letters to take prisoners who they think are too aloof down a peg or two.

Some prisoners will listen to an officer and then go up to a woman and say, 'Your old man . . . so and so . . .' and the woman will say, 'How do you know?.' 'Miss So-and-So told me.' And the woman has been going round telling everyone how much her old man loves her, just to keep herself together. But now she thinks, 'If the officer has told *her*, how many others has she told?' On the other hand, if anything really bad has happened no one tells you about it. That's the main concern of women in prison, they can't get any information. Once an officer made a remark to me about a woman's letter: 'Look what her old man's saying, that'll take the smile off her face.' I was cleaning the letter office at the time and the officer was talking about a woman who held her head high, tried to keep her dignity together. Okay, she did look snotty, but she was holding on to something, for God's sake. And this officer was delighted that her husband had written to say he was having an affair with her sister!

I've also seen prison officers winding women up on visits. A friend of mine was married to an Iranian, a really handsome guy. When he came on visits, one particular prison officer would stand just behind them. Then, when the visit was over she would make sure that she escorted the husband out of the visiting room, making sure too that she could be seen smiling at and joking with him. My friend would go 'Josie, I could kill her,' and I'd say, 'She's doing it on purpose.' 'I know,' she'd reply, 'cos she's always commenting about him. "Isn't your man a nice-looking guy? What's he doing all the time while you're in here?."' But you couldn't accuse them of anything because you'd be called paranoid, same as when they made remarks about your weight, about how fat you're getting. If you went to anyone and complained about being wound-up like that it would be, 'You're paranoid!' They use children an awful lot too. For instance, if a woman went off into one [began to shout and scream] they'd bring an officer along who knew all about her and they'd stand there and say, 'How's your little girl? She's a beautiful little girl. Make it easier for us — think of your kid.'

With every part of the prisoners' lives laid open for inspection in a constant round of body searches, strip searches and cell searches, prisoners have little enough space in which to keep themselves together, to hold on to some sense of identity. None the less some prisoners do try to maintain an illusion of privacy within their cells. It is an illusion which costs them dearly each time there is a cell search and an illusion which makes them terribly vulnerable to the worst excesses of prison officers' vindictiveness. When, however, two officers made the mistake of winding-up Josie's cell-mate during a cell search, they got more than they had bargained for. In the following account we can see how the combination of petty rules, officer arbitrariness and officer vindictiveness resulted in a most unfortunate injury to an officer.

As I said, the way you get treated depends on whether you have many contacts outside, whether you have letters and visits. But you could get punished just for having a teaspoon in your cell: they would actually write out a report to the Governor and you would be expected to go before her and make excuses for yourself — when it's all so unreal. You feel you're totally naked to them, that there's nothing you can keep away from them. At the same time, every inmate has something which she shouldn't in her cell, whether its boot polish, an extra deodorant, a teaspoon or whatever. So if there's to be a cell search you get rid of it all because you know that unless they find anything really illegal they will actually nick you for a little teaspoon. If, for instance, they found an ounce of dope in your cell, then obviously the teaspoon and the deodorant wouldn't matter, but if they did nick you for the teaspoon that could be four days' non-smoking, which means an awful lot to a real smoker, especially in prison.

They told us we were to have a cell search at nine-twenty. They came to the cell, stripped off each individual blanket, shook them and threw them outside the door. Jeannette and I were sitting on chairs outside the cell. You're supposed to be watching them all the time, but obviously if they go round the corner you can't always see them. The woman I was sharing with had been a junkie for fifteen years and her child was actually born addicted to heroin. Six months later her husband had died from an overdose of heroin. I knew that this had all meant a lot to her and I knew also that it was all on record, so that the prison officers knew about it too. After they've been through your bedding, your clothing and your letters they get down to your photographs. She had photos of her child, Emily, and they began to rip off their cardboard frames. Their excuse is that the cardboard outlines the photograph and that you could have slid a packet of dope behind it. It was a total wind-up because they knew they hadn't found anything. They knew that the only thing that would hurt Jeannette was to have a go at the child. I knew it too, because it would choke me up the way Jeannette would pick up that photo every night and say, "Night my Emily, I love you.' That photo was also part of her husband who had died.

The officers knew *exactly* what they were doing. When they touched the photos Jeannette was off her chair in a moment. I said, 'Jeannette, don't. That's what they want you to do.' I knew what she was feeling and I knew that I was going to get involved in it too. I knew that they were wrong and I knew that they were angry that they couldn't find anything in that cell. At last they were just dumping everything with disgust. They were pulling faces and going, 'Yuk!' when they flung the underwear out of the door. Then they read our letters, nudging each other and sniggering. All the time I was begging Jeannette, 'Don't let them win; if you lose your temper, they win.' They finished the cell search, everything was outside in the corridor and the cell was bare, apart from the beds and the wardrobe. They had not won.

I then went through the strip search procedure. My way of getting past the embarrassment of being actually naked in front of someone who is fully clothed is to look them in the eye, look down at my own body, then look at theirs and go, 'Yeh, it's alright, innit?' (Incidentally, it had taken me years to learn that if I could make comments like that I could get away with them.) That all finished I was just picking up an

ashtray which was full when one of the prison officers picked
up a dustbin and slammed it into my arm, so that all the ash
went over my bed linen. At that same moment a landing
officer walked round the corner. I began to flip. I went,
'There's no need for that, you didn't fucking have to do that.'
She said, 'I was only going to empty your bin.' I said, 'Yeh . . .
and since when did officers empty inmates' bins?' The landing
officer then came up and said, 'Look Josie, leave this to me.
I'll sort this out. I'll get you clean sheets.' And I trusted her.
She was a straight one. And she looked at the officer as much
as to say, 'And I'll have something to say to you in the office.'
But then the other one, the one who had ripped Jeannette's
photo, said, 'I shouldn't bother, they're used to living in filth.'
And then I did flip. It was the straw that broke the camel's
back. I slammed my fist down on the table, it upturned and
this prison officer who was about six foot four grabbed my
wrist and our heads collided — bang! Later they were to tell
me that I'd broken her nose. I just said, 'That's a load of
bollocks, and you know it.' She had to spend three days in
hospital but that was one of those things. After all, if it had
been *my* nose the story to the Governor would have been 'Oh
well, Madam, that was done while we were restraining her.'
That time, as it happened, it was the other way round.

When prison officers engage in 'winding-up', their general aim is to
provoke prisoners into doing themselves an injury. '**Setting-up**', as
we are using the term here, is that even more pernicious activity
whereby prison officers provoke one or more of the prisoners into
attacking another prisoner. This is a common feature of imprisonment and women's prisons provide no exception.

You'd get an inmate come on the wing and prisoners would
say, 'Who's the new girl, Miss?' And they'd say, 'Oh . . . you
don't want to bother with her. I can't tell you why. You'll find
out soon enough.' So they obviously didn't approve of what
the new inmate had done and then you'd go round asking.
Eventually you'd find out and one of the young ones would
go in and beat her up and it would be the very same officer
who had told her what the inmate was in for who would then
be putting her on report. But all the time she was on report

the officers would be really nice to her, she would get a cushy time on punishment. So if you beat up the nonce cases (the term for those who're in for doing children or old people), you got more credit from the officers. But if you were friendly with a nonce case you got black marks. I've heard prison officers make comments like, 'She's a friend of that nonce case, she can wait for her letter till tea-time.' Likewise, if any woman (not a nonce case) was upset and screaming the officers would let her carry on until it really began to annoy everyone else because they hoped that you'd all get together and go round and tell the screaming inmate to shut up. I never actually fell for that one . . . though I fell for a few others.

In fact it was in Holloway that Josie was very badly set-up. At the age of nineteen she was selected to be yet another in the line of prisoners who, over the years, have been set-up to attack Myra Hindley.

At the time I was serving three years and I was nineteen. It happened when they moved Myra Hindley onto my wing. I knew who she was but I didn't know the details of the case because it was such a long time ago. About two Sundays after she had been on the wing an article about her was published in *The News of The World*. The Deputy Governor had said that the article shouldn't be issued to us. He asked to see Myra and when she had gone off to see him I got taken into the office by the prison officer who was then in charge of the wing and another prison officer. They sat me behind the door, opened out this two-page spread and said, 'Read that.' It was quite a disturbing newspaper article. As I read it one officer stood near the door so that the article could be quickly whipped away if anyone came in. (At the age of nineteen I used to feel completely loyal to my D-wing officers — it wasn't until after my three-year sentence that I realized that prison officers didn't actually give a damn about me at all.)

Anyhow, I read this whole article and because what I had read had made me shake and tremble with horror they took me for a walk round the prison grounds. When I got back it was dinner-time, so I went up to the recess to the loo, came out and was washing my hands, when I heard someone coming up the stairs. It was Myra. I thought, 'I'll just stay here until she goes by.' But she didn't go by, she came on across the bridge. Apparently, she had been talking to the officers and she had actually been kept in the office until they knew I was in the recess. It had been all set up. It was almost immediately after I had read that newspaper article and I just couldn't handle the horror of what I'd read . . . so I went for her.

It took the prison officers an awful long time to answer the alarm bell, and by that time she was quite a mess. I'd knocked her teeth loose at the front, she had to eat through a straw for about six weeks. Her nose was crossed to the left side of her face, I'd split her lip, her knee and her ear, and she had two black eyes. The officers treated me like a celebrity. It was: 'Here's half an ounce of tobacco, Josie;' 'Let me shake your hand;' 'Well done Josie, I've waited twelve years for someone to do that' etc. It wasn't until the Assistant Governor came down that I realized I had done something wrong. I was way up in the air with all the praise that the officers had heaped on me and then Miss McCollum came down on me like a ton of bricks. I realized then what I'd done, though I didn't realize till later that I'd been set up. The Assistant Governor knew that there had been instigators but I wouldn't tell her who had shown me the article. All the time I was in the annexe I was loving the attention. I had a radio, sugar, stuff from the canteen. If Miss McCollum had known about it she would have stopped it, that's for sure.

It wasn't until I had been in the annexe about six weeks that I began to get little doubts. Myra was high up in the prison hierarchy and to her face the prison officers were always very nice, as they were to anyone high up in the hierarchy. I had been before the Board of Visitors and lost one hundred and ten days remission and done ten days solitary confinement before I realized . . . 'They're really nice to her face, yet behind her back they tell me that they hate her.' And that began to really get me . . . if they were doing that to her . . . they would do it to others . . . they would do it to me.

Surviving Bleak House, Styal

Josie first went to Styal to serve a Young Prisoner sentence.

> Styal fits the stereotype of the ideal prison. The Styal prison
> officers push you to the point where you have either to stand
> up and fight back or bow down and scrub that floor for the
> fifth or fifteenth time. They are not allowed to be friendly to
> inmates and every so often, somewhere in a corner of the
> prison, the whole thing just erupts into violence. They have
> their Muppet Wing [for women who are mentally disturbed
> or retarded] same as Holloway has its Muppet Wing and
> they've got their punishment block, Bleak House. The men
> run Bleak House at the weekends and, if you wanted a
> tampax then, you had to ask a male officer.
>   I'd heard so much about Styal that I actually escaped from
> Pucklechurch two days before I was supposed to go there.
> When I eventually went to Styal I was still on punishment for
> escaping, so I went straight to Bleak House. They dope you
> up to the eyeballs if they take you anywhere in case there is
> any sort of incident on the way, so by the time I got to Bleak
> from Bristol I was fairly shattered. Bleak is quite frightening
> from the word go. You don't get your mattress until nine
> o'clock in the evening. If you're lucky you've got a bed; if not
> it's just a mattress on the floor job. When I arrived that first
> day I lay down on the springs of the bed with my coat half
> under and half over me and promptly fell asleep. Next thing I
> knew, the door had opened and an officer was screaming at
> me that I would get an extra day down there if I should fall
> asleep again. That was a Styal rule, that you mustn't sleep
> during the day.
>   If you're on loss of privileges, you're not allowed books,
> only the Bible. The heating is kept really low, so low that I
> used to do running on the spot to keep warm. You're not
> allowed to sing or whistle and, as I was to discover, even
> feeding the squirrels could be an offence. One day I was
> feeding a squirrel with a bit of bread through the window, it
> was the highlight of my day — I'd spent a long time getting
> him to come and get it from my fingers — when suddenly the

door was opened, then slammed shut. (They love slamming
doors.) I was charged with offending against good order and
discipline by encouraging vermin and I got ten days loss of
privileges. People were terrified of Bleak House. I've seen big
grown women sobbing, begging and pleading with prison
officers to let them out. When you're in punishment in
Holloway you're attached to a wing, you can hear people, see
them walking about. In Bleak House no one can see you at
all. It has a very inhuman feel to it. Once I was in a cell which
should not have been in use. It was damp, cold and wet. One
day when there were visitors to Bleak I heard the officers
take my name card off the door. I said, 'What are you doing
with my card?' Then I clicked. It was the Visiting Magistrate
who had gone by and they had taken my card out so that he
wouldn't know anyone was in that cell. I never had any
visitors all the time I was in Styal, so apart from those officers
no one knew I existed. During the time they had removed my
card from the door I didn't officially exist at all and that is
just another way of dying in prison.

The next time Josie went to Styal was after the Myra Hindley
incident. After the Styal reception officers had successfully pulled
off a wind-up job which landed Josie in Bleak House for her first
three days at Styal, she was moved to Hooker House, a house for
the more difficult prisoners. Just before Christmas, however, she
was involved in a further incident and she was sent once more to
Bleak House. Unbeknown to her at the time, Josie was to stay in
solitary confinement in Bleak House for six long months. This time
the authorities were out to break her.

They found me guilty of fighting with another inmate —
fourteen days behind the door. I said 'Look, I've never
pleaded not guilty before because I've always been guilty
when I've been on report. But I'm not guilty this time. I
pleaded not guilty because I *am* not guilty.' 'But we find you
guilty,' she said with a smile (they always say it with a smile).
So, I went into one, because I didn't want to be locked up
over Christmas for something I hadn't done. But of course
they did lock me up over Christmas and it was a Christmas I
shall never forget.

On Christmas Eve the prison choir came round singing *Silent Night*. When I heard *Silent Night* I had a big lump in my throat and I burst into tears. The Chief came down and gave me four cigarettes but I hadn't got any matches and I couldn't ask for any because I had lost my privileges. Then they let me out to have a bath. As I walked back to tell the officer that I'd finished my bath a flap on a cell came down and I looked through. A woman had tried to commit suicide and was sitting there in a big heap — a *heap*, not a pool — of blood, from where she had cut an artery in her leg. I wanted desperately to help but — it was Christmas Eve remember and a woman had just attempted to commit suicide — all they were concerned about was getting *me* into *my* cell before they opened *her* door! That's getting your priorities right, isn't it?

After my fourteen days was up they came to me and said that I must go before the Governor to *ask* to come off punishment! The actual wording is, 'Madam, my punishment is finished, can I go back on a house, please?' I actually went before the Governor and said, 'Throw the key away, throw the key away, because I aint askin' you for nothin! I didn't ask for my punishment and I'm not asking to come off it. It's the only prison in this country that I've been to where you have to *ask* to come off punishment. You gave me fourteen days punishment, either you take me off it or you leave me on it.' I then walked back to my cell and I stayed there for six months. I just got worse from then on. I became convinced that they were doing something to my food, because of the way they used to give it to me with a knowing nod and a wink, saying 'Enjoy your dinner, Josie' and grinning. The night officer would bang on my door at any time of the night. Sometimes during the day I'd be sitting on the floor with no mattress, no chair, no nothing and my door would slam open and in they'd run, male officers too, drag me to the strips and literally kick seven sorts of shit out of me. Sometimes, not always, they would get a nurse down to give me an injection. And I used to sit in the strip cells wondering what I was supposed to have done; whether I'd gone off my head so much that I'd done something really bad and didn't know about it. One day I was in my cell, hugging my knees, rocking myself and looking at the wall, when I thought I saw a daddy-long-legs on the plaster. When I looked closer it wasn't a daddy-long-legs but a piece of somebody's scalp. I pulled it off with my fingers and it was total horror as I realized what I'd got hold of. I thought, 'Oh my God . . .' I don't think I was really right in my head for a long time after that.

I got worse and worse. I used to go off into spaces somewhere in my head, to places where no one else could ever reach me. They used to open my door and put my food in and I'd not even notice. I'd come back from some place in my head and I'd think, 'How long has that been there?' and I'd realize that it was stone-cold and must have been there for hours. Yet if I hadn't withdrawn into my head I would have gone completely crazy because they were trying to wind me up. I knew that there was nothing more they could do to me physically — apart from killing me — and subconsciously I also realized that if I could remove myself from them mentally then they wouldn't be able to drive me crazy and put me in Broadmoor, either.

No one intervened in Josie's situation until she was in such a state of debilitation that it was decided to transfer her to Pucklechurch for a welfare visit with her family. The visit never did come off but at least Josie, in being transferred to Pucklechurch, had received a temporary reprieve from the tortures of Bleak House. She was determined never to return there. She would die first.

When I arrived at Pucklechurch I couldn't go out on exercise, I couldn't communicate with people and I couldn't hold a conversation. I literally could only say 'Yes', 'No' or nod. I was in such a state that a welfare visit would have been quite out of the question anyway. It was the Chief Officer who came in to tell me that I wasn't going to get the welfare visit. She said, 'You've got to go back to Styal.' I had known that woman since I was fourteen but I couldn't answer her when she said that. I could no longer put the words together. The doctor came in to 'fit' me for transfer. I said 'Transfer? Where?' He said, 'Styal'. I just stood up and went . . . BOSH! I head-butted the wall, knocked myself out cold and when I woke up the doctor said, 'What's happening? I've never known you to hurt yourself like this before. What psychiatrist are you seeing in Styal?' I said, 'I don't see one. They've never offered to let me see one. I'm in a cell on my own and I see only prison officers who insult me.' He said, 'How were you getting on at Holloway?' I told him that I had been seeing a psychologist there who had shown me videos of how my behaviour looked to other people and that what she had been saying had been making sense. The doctor said, 'Well, that sounds more productive. I'm going to ring the Home Office and see if I can get you medically transferred back to Holloway.' So he did. The Home Office said that they didn't mind so long as the Governor of Holloway agreed. I waited five hours in agony before I knew the answer. During that five hours I decided that I would go for the steering wheel and crash the car if they took me back to Styal. There was no way they were getting me back there alive because I knew they would kill me and I didn't want to die that way. If I was going to die it was going to be a death of my own choosing. It wouldn't be by being kicked to death in a strip cell in Bleak House.

The Chief came to me at last and said, 'You're going to Holloway tomorrow.' But it didn't allay the anxiety and worry I was feeling. It was not until we got to Reading that I really believed that we were *en route* for Holloway, and not half-way up the M1 to Styal.

This was 1977. I had gone to Styal weighing about twelve-and-a-half stone and I had come back weighing eight. I saw the psychologist for nearly a whole day, three times a week. She had to start from scratch and gradually I was getting somewhere. I could have a conversation again, I could queue up in the canteen without freaking out and then they began to take me out to walk in the Holloway Road. But it was a slow process. Sometimes I just couldn't handle being out of my cell and I'd wreck things so that they would have to lock me up again. After a few months, however, I began to feel more positive and so relieved, in fact, to find that my head hadn't gone for good that I began to function normally again. On 5 October 1977 I was paroled and, having absolutely nowhere else to go, I went into a bed-sitter which had been found for me just round the corner from the prison. At last I

was out of the prison — and I was living in the same street as
the prison officers!

Surviving Psychiatry

At fourteen they said I was emotionally disturbed. At sixteen
I had a personality disorder. At seventeen I had psychopathic
tendencies. By eighteen I was a fully graduated psychopath.
At twenty-one I was a paranoid schizophrenic.

Not many prisoners to whom we have spoken have much time for
prison psychiatry. To begin with it is difficult for prisoners to have
respect for *any* of the prison professionals who walk by on the
other side when women prisoners are being more forcibly
restrained than might be necessary, who ask no questions about
unusual degrees of bruising, who do not intervene when women
are being kept in solitary confinement for days on end.
Additionally, prisoners find psychiatrists authoritarian and blinkered,
always looking for some flaw in the prisoner's make-up rather than
at those more immediate causes of tension to be found in the
prison regime itself.

The psychiatrist had no idea. He was always absolutely right,
he was never wrong. He was in fact *always* wrong about me
because at that time my behaviour was caused by my attempts
to climb up, to be someone in the prison structure itself. No
one actually bothered to find out *why* you did the things you
did. To the prison officer you would be a vicious bastard, to
the Governor and everyone else you would be sick and the
psychiatrist always knew everything in any case — so he
didn't need to find out. I was usually given psychiatric labels
on the basis of fifteen-minute interviews. They ask for your
life story and you've said it so many times that it just comes
off pat; of course you say it without feeling — and there you
are! Labelled psychopath!
No one asks you about the crime. No one asks you about
prison. They always asked me about my early life but not
about what had happened to me in those institutions, since
the age of fourteen. And, personally, I think it was those
institutions which were responsible for what happened from

then on. I never knew anything *except* institutions. No one
took me out and said, 'Look this is the real world, let's go
slowly, let's help you.' No one mentioned any kind of social
problem. It was just me. According to psychiatrists I was
either crazy or bad. It was always 'What's wrong with Josie?'
Not, 'What's wrong with prison?'

Viewing psychiatrists as being either irrelevant or ineffectual not
many prisoners get into any sort of serious dialogue with them. So,
as long as they can avoid being sent to Broadmoor, prisoners do
not find that psychiatrists themselves pose a serious threat to their
survival. The *drugs* which psychiatrists can (and do) prescribe,
however, pose a threat of an entirely different magnitude.

Surviving Drugs

The question of drug usage in women's prisons is a thorny one.
Many women have been prescribed (some people would say over-
prescribed) heavy doses of drugs for years prior to their sentences.
If the prison doctor then stops prescribing drugs which the women
have been legitimately prescribed outside s/he is likely to be
accused of being punitive. If, on the other hand, s/he continues to
prescribe large doses of drugs then s/he is likely to be accused of
drugging women solely for penal control purposes. The pains and
tensions of imprisonment itself are such that it is not surprising
that drugs illegitimately obtained and retained are the prized
currency of illicit prison barter systems.

You put it into your mouth, hold it there and then you either
spit it into the mouth of the person who wants it or spit it into
a container.

Nor is it surprising that young girls cooped-up and tensed-up
beyond endurance should see drugs as a panacea for all their
several ills of boredom, routine, tension, frustration, anxiety and
the nagging sense of prison-induced nothingness.

When my friend and me were having a competition to see
who could get the most drugs at Pucklechurch I was

prescribed so many drugs that I got lock-jaw and my tongue swelled up so that I couldn't speak.

What *is* surprising, the above examples of illicit drug usage notwithstanding, is that it could be argued on the basis of the 1982 Prison Report that, in 1982, in the women's penal establishments the dosage rate of drugs affecting the central nervous system was extremely high, with Holloway at the top of the list with a dosage rate of 365 doses per woman per year.[5] Of course, the same Report (p. 60) is right to warn us that the figures given cannot be regarded as a precision tool for monitoring the quantities and types of drugs administered. It is, none the less, safe to assume that although some women will have obviously had *no* drugs at all whilst in prison, others will have consumed very large quantities indeed. Women like Josie who have been in and out of institutions since either childhood or early adolescence may have already been damaged by the large amounts of drugs which they have been prescribed to ease the pains of imprisonment. For many women are unsuspecting of the permanent adverse effects which such heavy drug consumption might engender, especially if the drugs have been legitimately obtained from a doctor. The effects can, in fact, range from permanent overweight through all kinds of motor impairment to a permanent dependency upon drugs.

Women don't get anything in prison, no trades, nothing. You just sit around taking medicine, getting fat, worrying about getting fat, eating more and taking more medicine because you're getting fat — it's a vicious circle. Some women go in weighing eight stone and come out weighing thirteen stone. They take hundreds of Largactil and — Phew! — they go up like balloons in a very short time. Then you see them eighteen months after they've got out and they haven't shed a pound. Their pupils are massive, they're speeding out of their heads and they can't shift that weight. It's had a lasting effect on them. If you're really overweight you know you are; and every time you sit and look at yourself in the bath you know you are. You look and you think, 'That comes from prison.'

Josie herself put on an immense amount of weight as a result of

drugs given to her in Pucklechurch and whilst at Holloway she
suffered adverse effects from the drug Haloperidol.

I was put on a drug called Haloperidol and I lost all my co-
ordination. The drugs didn't make me dopey but I just
couldn't lift my arm up and down to clean my teeth or brush
my hair. I'd put food into my mouth and forget to chew it and
then when I opened my mouth to speak the food fell out.
They didn't really know me then at Holloway. They had
previously only seen me for a week. I said to them, 'Look I'm
not like this really. I can cope on the wing without drugs.' But
I had taken the drugs originally because they had insisted
that they were good for me. They don't actually force drugs
on you so in the end I just refused them. Some of the women
obviously need the drugs, but excessive amounts make you
so zombified that you feel that you're awake but dead, that
when you're standing you want to sit, that when you're in
your cell you want to be out and so on. I knew that it wasn't
me, that it was the drugs — but that's just another way of
going under when you're in prison. The real horror is that no
one takes any notice of you, that you can't make anyone
listen because you're absolutely drugged out of your head
and that they, and you, know it.

Losing Modes

Though this is a record of survival, the main thrust of the chapter
so far has been to delineate in all its complexity the minefield of
psychological and physical threats to survival which confront the
women residing in Her Majesty's Prisons and other penal
institutions. Yet, historically, stories of imprisonment, at the same
time as documenting the worst tortures which people have ever
devised for each other, have also provided perennial testimony to
the creativity, durability, humour, courage and compassion of the
human spirit. All of these qualities are to be found in the women's
prisons. Before we turn to them, however, we wish to underline
our arguments concerning the more dominant, oppressive and
officially-inspired face of women's imprisonment by describing the
penalties for *failing* to survive.

Death is obviously the ultimate price to be paid physically by those whose strategies to survive imprisonment are unsuccessful. Upon her last release from prison one of Josie's first calls was to the Women In Prison office to report that she and other prisoners feared for the life of a young prisoner who was continiously hurling herself at the walls of her cell in Holloway's C1 Psychiatric Unit and who had been seen with large lumps and lacerations on her forehead. Sights and sounds like these are commonplace in the women's prisons and Borstals and are warning enough to tough and determined young women like Josie that they had better take care of themselves. Others, who may not have been so physically, mentally and emotionally strong to begin with, pay the price for weakness with their lives. The issues surrounding prison deaths have been fully discussed elsewhere (see note 4) and we do not intend to discuss them further now. Suffice it here to stress that, in any discussion of the penalties incurred as a result of a failure to survive imprisonment, it must always be remembered that *death* is both the ultimate physical penalty for those who *do not* survive and the ever-present fear of those who *do*. Other fears are of institutionalization, mutilation, injury and — in payment of the ultimate psychological penalty — madness.

Institutionalization refers to that phenomenon wherein some people who have lived in institutions for a long time find it difficult to live outside them. But the process of institutionalization is not entirely a passive one, something that is merely *done to* the prisoner. In an unequal society like the UK, where so many women prisoners have nothing at all going for them on the outside, the 'institution', oppressive as it is, can provide the only psychological and physical shelter where they are known, where they have any positive identity and credit whatsoever. Awareness of this concomitant commitment to and rejection of the institution, however, can bewilder and embitter prisoners, making it even more difficult for them to make sense of themselves, their imprisonment, their pasts and their futures.

> Everybody talked big about 'when I get out of here' even though they knew damn well that they were going to come back because there was nothing out there for them anyway. But they had to talk like that; you had to give this sort of talk even though you knew that when it came to it you didn't

actually want to go! You could never admit to *that*; that was the hardest thing to admit, that you had got to the stage where you actually liked it there! What was the point of fighting, what was the point of fucking the system, singing anti-screw songs, stumping up and down, glaring at them, using up all that energy . . . if you actually liked it there? No one could make sense of that, so no one ever admitted it.

Josie, paroled from Holloway when she had barely recovered from her six months' solitary incarceration in Bleak House, Styal, found that she had to move from the accommodation which had been found for her in the street just round the corner from the prison because she was forever tantalised by the prison officers' living testimony to the fact that she was no longer part of their working lives — and that their working lives were part of the only world where she had ever felt that she was someone.

At first it was a novelty to have a bed-sit in the same road as the prison officers. I queued up behind them in the off-licence, went to the same launderette and saw them everytime I came out of my door. But I missed the attention. They were there but I had no claim on their attention any more. I couldn't handle that situation so I moved away. It was probably just as well that I did because I don't think I could have lasted much longer without doing something to get myself back in. I would have been back in Holloway, and with the total intent of being there.

Josie took avoidance action to prevent the most extreme effect of institutionalization, the committing of a crime with the deliberate intent of returning to the institution, but she is well aware that the marks of the prison can be inscribed in a woman's psyche for a long time after the prison gate has clanged behind her for the last time.

When you come out, after years inside, you look at the world as you have known it and you think 'This is how it is, and this is how it's going to be.' You don't expect much, and it's safer to be that way. You're used to living the image of the big, tough criminal so you go round talking like that. You meet

others like you, in the tube and the dole queue and you all
talk the same language — a language that you all understand
but which none of you want any part of at another level.
You're in a different place, a different atmosphere but you
slip into the prison gear. It goes on and on affecting your life.
Every so often I find myself relating to outside just as I did in
prison. It's only now, after almost a year, that I'm starting to
relate to things in my own way, rather than in a conditioned
way. When I came out I actually had a conditioned response
to everything and that was the safest way for me to be. But
now I try to stop myself, and I watch myself and I think,
'Turn it off. That comes from prison.'

'Cutting' and other forms of self-mutilation are common responses
to the pains and the tensions, to the emotional and the sexual
deprivations experienced by women and girls in prison.

The prison does so much to people that they can't hit back all
the time. They get to the stage where they can't even justify
anything to themselves any more so they turn it in on
themselves. Me, I could hit back, I could smash up the cell,
but some women can't do that. Maybe they are afraid of the
punishment block; maybe they are afraid of being handled
roughly by the prison officers; maybe they would see it as
giving in if they *did* smash up . . . so the only thing left to them
is to hurt themselves. The same things that caused me to
smash my cell or wreck the whole wing cause these women to
cut themselves. It's called 'cutting'. I've seen horrific
mutilations. Some prisoners just scratch themselves with pins;
some swallow safety pins or bits of glass. I've even known
women swallow batteries and bed-springs. Personally, I've
never done it, but it happens so often that you could call it an
epidemic.

Women who 'cut-up' get little sympathy from the authorities. The
prison officers attempt to turn the other prisoners against the
prisoner who causes a nuisance by 'cutting-up'.

They would lock us all up while they dealt with it. You would
be sitting in your cell waiting to come out for association and

you'd wonder why they hadn't unlocked your door. You'd say, 'Why aren't we getting association?' 'Oh, Cathy so-and-so has just cut-up and we're having to deal with it,' they'd reply. With some women it could happen so much that you'd even begin to think, 'Fucking inconvenience, that's really out of order.' But that's what the officers wanted you to feel, so that you would go round and say, 'Because of you we've been locked up.' But that would have been doing the officers' job for them and I wouldn't have that. The officers just thought that anyone who cut-up was a complete and utter waste of time and they made it so that every time anyone cut-up it was an absolute piss-off for all the other prisoners. Nobody ever asked the woman *why* she'd done it.

It is widely believed by women prisoners that some prison doctors are equally unsympathetic.

The only attention they get is being stitched up. If she's smashed something to cut herself with then she's nicked. But if she's just used something that she's come across then all that happens is that an injury form is filled in. Many prisoners have told me that they believe that doctors haven't given them anaesthetic while they have been stitching them. It must be a punishment, mustn't it? It takes longer to stitch up than it does to slash open. Imagine stitching someone without anaesthetic! Women have told me that they believe that the doctor's attitude must be, 'You did it, now you can have it stitched up on our terms or not at all.' Imagine doing that to a woman who is already desperate!

Madness, or at least the spectre of madness, lurks as a constant fear in the minds of many women in prison. Threats to their sanity are made from so many sides that even the toughest women fear that one day they will break. Being alone in cellular confinement is one most testing time and even if women find that they can cope with punishment it is not long before they begin to wonder if their very coping with solitary confinement is not abnormal in itself. This state of unreality, of no longer being able to trust oneself, is one of the most typical and feared of prison-induced states.

Until I was nineteen the time I spent locked up in a cell was a killer. I had to sit there with the person I hated most of all — myself! Ten minutes seemed like four hours. I'd scratch the walls and kick the pot round the cell just to make a noise. Then, gradually, I got so used to it that I couldn't come out any more. I'd actually ask them to lock me up. After six months in Bleak I thought I'd damaged my head for good. They never allow for the fact that all the time you're in prison you're balancing on a tightrope. You can either stay on it or you can go down. The medical authorities should overrule the discipline authorities but the doctors are not really very interested. The doctor in Styal should have seen that I was wasting away in body and in mind but all he did was to throw open the door, say 'Fit?' and I wouldn't even answer him, I was so far away. The door would be opening all the time: food, slop-out, doctor, Visiting Magistrate, Governor — and in the end it just wasn't registering with me. They most probably thought I was being ignorant, but in the end, I just wasn't there with them any more. When I did register them I just thought, 'Fucking well leave me alone. I've had enough.' Though I still wouldn't give in.

Through a mixture of determination and a very few lucky breaks Josie survived. Others whom we know have not been so fortunate.

There is Pamela who spent four months in Bleak and she just can't hold anything together. I was telling her yesterday about when I was working in reception in Holloway when she came back there from Styal. She said that she couldn't remember me being there. I said, 'Well I remember you, Pam. You were on all fours barking and snapping like a dog and the prison officers told me to open your door and kick the dinner in because you might bite me. I wouldn't agree to that. I said to them, "You open the door and I'll put it in." And I'll be honest with you, Pam, I really thought you were going to bite me.' I was totally horrified and frightened. They'd treated her like an animal and there she was acting like one. Once I had reminded her of it all she told me that in Bleak she had gone to extremes — covered herself with semolina, gravy etc. just so that they would have to open the door and clean her up. Some women cover themselves with shit for the same reason. It's not so surprising. When everything else has been taken away from them it's all they have left to fight with. Some people go totally off their heads. One woman whom I knew when she first came into prison was totally OK, a very strong woman. After three or four years of being shipped around different prisons she was completely unrecognizable. When I was last inside it took me three or four weeks to recognize her. She used to come into the exercise yard talking to herself, raving out of a Bible. When she had begun her sentence she had been totally together, now she's totally off her head — in a world of her own.

Some women finish up in Broadmoor, like my friend Julie. She was my best friend, a very strong woman. Then, after she'd spent months in solitary confinement in Durham and even longer in Bleak on punishment, I suddenly heard that she'd set her cell on fire, cut her legs open, cut her throat, cut her stomach, set her jeans on fire. They were things she would never have done when we were Borstal girls together. But she had been battered and bruised into submission by prison officers for so long that in the end she was swallowed up by the system itself — and sent to Broadmoor.

Winning Modes

When I was younger they were trying to teach me a lesson and I responded with total violence. That was the only way I knew. Now it's different because I can use the system against itself. I know now what *I* can get away with and I know what *they* can get away with.

Josie has not spent eight years of her life in Her Majesty's Prisons and other penal institutions without learning how they work. She has seen both the unacceptable face of official coercion and the variety of ways in which prisoners counter it. Young girls are apt to meet violence with violence. As women get older they learn to buck the system at less cost to themselves. In a situation where they have been denuded of almost all privacy, all legitimate channels of complaint against injustice and where official violence has engendered in some of them an understandable hatred of prison officers, prisoners have to fight with whatever weapons come to hand. It is in getting back at officers that the more spirited prisoners can share those moments of hilarious and mirthful complicity which both cement friendships and give prisoners back some degree of control of their situation.

> I always needed someone to make me laugh. I had a friend called Tiddler who was a real comedienne. We played juvenile tricks just for a laugh. We'd mix the officers' salt and sugar together. One prison officer used to eat prisoners' left-over meals which she wasn't supposed to do. We'd cut the top off the puddings and insert things from the swill bin. It got to the stage where what was going in was really disgusting. If we could get hold of them we would spit on any officers' cups that were lying around. When people like me and Jeannette were in the kitchen they wouldn't usually give us coffee-cups to wash or allow us to make coffee for them, but once we got hold of a whole trayful when an officer who didn't know us was on duty. We did wash them. Then, before we made the coffee, we stuck our fingers up our bums and smeared all the inside rims of the cups. Then we watched them drink from them, saying to ourselves, 'Kiss my arse now!' I know it sounds disgusting, it probably *is* disgusting but there's no bigger thrill than to get your own back on people who've got almost total power over you and who are constantly abusing it. 'Kiss my arse,' I thought. 'That's just what you're doing now.' We were in hysterics.

The whole point of survival for the young Borstal girls who foresee a certain inevitability in their progress through the penal system is to become a top dog — the 'Governor' of a wing, a star at the top of the prison hierarchy. Josie succeeded in her aim to get to the top.

> I climbed the ladder when I was young, but after that my reputation went before me. The reputation was based on causing the riots at Bullwood, being frightened of nobody and nothing. Plus I was the one who'd done Myra Hindley.
> During the last two sentences I was the smart-arse, the

clever bastard, because they couldn't nick me for anything. They *knew* I was dealing in dope, baronning in tobacco, but they couldn't nick me for it. I was no longer down in punishment saying, 'I won't,' and getting shit knocked out of me. I was up there in a cell. I was no longer bouncing off them, hurting myself. They had taught me so well how to use their system that by then I could use it for myself, against them. I became the 'heavy' of the whole prison, not just my wing.

At the top, Josie was in a position where she could not only buck the system but also redress some of the wrongs which she saw officers committing against other, weaker prisoners.

You're either seen as a good top person or a bad top person. For instance, I could insist that an ill woman be taken up in a lift and not made to walk up the stairs — because the officers knew that if I sat down the whole wing would sit down with me. Things like that I could do because I was the 'biggy' the 'Momma' of the wing.

In fact, and as is usual when people are placed together in extreme situations, Josie made some good friendships in prison.

There are some brilliant friendships made in prison. One woman who had been in Holloway for such a long time used to come up to my room, have coffee and play songs on her guitar and I used to think it was wonderful that she would take time out for me, just a kid. She was just such a kind person that when she sang a song I'd often have tears in my eyes. It's such a hard, hard situation in prison, yet people like A. do survive and make time to think of others.

There would always be enough misery about for something to get you in the guts. Whatever happened on a big wing seemed to affect most people anyway. If somebody was upset, say somebody's father, mother, sister or brother had just died, everybody would be that little affected. There would be no loud laughter, everybody would take just a little bit of the pain to themselves and — somehow — it made it so that in the end the very person who was upset would be trying to cheer everyone else up. The women were really together then, each prisoner feeling a bit of what every other prisoner felt. That's the way it was.

Prison officers, however, do not like women to be too friendly with each other or to receive too much comfort from each other's love and affection. Sexual relations between prisoners are still frowned upon by the authorities, though many women prisoners themselves know that the warmth of their relationships with other prisoners is one (and sometimes the *only*) major source of sustenance for them during their imprisonment.

> Women need comfort and if you can get into a relationship in prison I, personally, think it's a good thing. It doesn't hurt to be comforted by another woman in prison, nobody should knock anyone for it. Yet it's a reportable offence! It's called L.A.; lesbian activities. You can actually be done for lesbian activities! If you're seen kissing another woman, hugging another woman, just comforting another woman who might be sobbing on your shoulder, the prison officer will look through the spy-hole, see you wrapped in each other's arms and yell down the landing as if you're doing something unspeakable. The officers are so very crude about it too. The two women might only be sitting on the edge of their bunks talking to each other, but the officers make it sound sordid — 'You two, get in your own beds.' If women prisoners can't show tenderness to each other, they won't get it from anyone else, nor is there any other outlet for those emotions in the whole system. Can you wonder that so many women prisoners turn either to violence or to self-mutilation?[6]

Costs of Survival

In 1983 a male prisoner serving his twelfth year of a life sentence wrote to Pat Carlen: 'I was very interested in your recent book about Cornton Vale women's prison. It was an eye-opener for me. Like most other male prisoners, I'd always thought that the ladies had it nice and easy, cooking each other's meals and doing each other's hair.'

Such a view of women's imprisonment is not an unusual one. In fact, when women's imprisonment is seriously discussed — and that does not happen very often — three stereotypes of women prisoners tend to be put forward. In the first, women prisoners are seen to be fallen madonnas; 'ordinary women' who, having lapsed once, have the intelligence and 'female decency' to do their sentences quietly. In the second, women prisoners are seen as being poor broken-down reeds, victims of circumstances beyond their control but nonetheless needing a 'discipline' setting in which to order their 'disordered' lives and personalities. In the third stereotype, one purveyed mainly by prison officers and police officers and referring primarily to the Borstal and ex-Borstal girls, women prisoners are presented as being totally and uncontrollably violent and hysterical, amenable to only the most draconian forms of discipline, constraint and pharmaceutical intervention. Of course, not one of these stereotypes even begins to *describe* the majority of female prisoners, let alone *explain* why the behaviour of some women prisoners may be violent. For in fact it may be safely assumed that, prior to their first arrival at the prisons and the Borstals, women criminals have little in common except the fact that they have been either suspected or convicted of some crime. Once they are caught up in the penal system, however, they all face the same penal machinery, albeit experiencing its depredations in many different ways. Some women do indeed serve their sentences quietly: either they are too worn out to fight any more; or, being only the one time or infrequently in prison, they choose to serve their sentences as quietly as they can before returning to otherwise satisfactory lives or, at the least, supportive backgrounds. These women are the prisoners who are unlikely to experience officer violence, though most of them will experience a thousand-and-one humiliations and injustices emanating from both the uses and the abuses of the prison rules. Other prisoners, like the older Josie, will do their sentences without too much trouble because they will have learned to manipulate the system to their own advantage. By far the largest group in the penal institutions are those young women, who (like the younger Josie) have spent so long in institutions that they have no one and nothing waiting for them on the outside. These are the women who bear the full force of the penal machinery's cutting edge. What we have done in this chapter is to organize the experiences of just *one* of those young women around the motif of 'survival' in order to indicate what *so many more* of them have to face once they get caught up in the modern care/penal machine.

In sum, we have sought to demonstrate that:

1   Women's closed prisons are violent, frightening and damaging places.

2   The sources of violence in the women's closed prisons inhere in the technologies of both physical and pharmaceutical control.

3   These technologies of control are mobilized against prisoners who neither outside the prison, nor within it, have access to any legitimate ways of effectively countering the prison authorities' abuse of power.

4   In the absence of both any legitimate grievance machinery and any legitimate ways of letting off steam, certain prisoners can only stave off their prison-induced fears of death, madness, institutionalization and general loss of identity by engaging in survival strategies which may at first sight appear to be either gratuitously violent or otherwise inexplicable.

The prisoner is left with both the damage and the costs. It is with Josie's assessment of the price which she has paid for her own survival that we end this chapter.

I think that if I'd given in I wouldn't have been half the person I am today. I really do think that I'm a better person for not giving in, I really do believe that. But I could have gone under. I was lucky really because instead of going down I came out with my head held high. But although I survived I do think that I have been damaged emotionally because of my prison experience. Sometimes my emotions are so mixed up that I don't know what I'm feeling. I can't say that I'm either feeling sad, or hurt or needing comfort — I just don't know. It may appear to be a hardened attitude but prison doesn't actually make you hard, it just makes you mask all those feelings. As far as my emotions are concerned prison has fucked me up. In prison, if you showed what pleased you they would take it away from you; if you showed what hurt you they would hurt you again with it. You learned to block it all off and then it became a knot inside you, a wound that gets worse, a wound that doesn't heal . . .

When you come out you don't expect much — and you don't get much. All you want to survive is what's left of yourself.

Postscript: I'm Living Now

On 6 March 1983 I was taken from Cookham Wood Prison to The Court of Criminal Appeal in the Strand. Only the day before I had been found not guilty by the jury at Snaresbrook Crown Court for the incident involving the prison officer, which was described on page 156 above.

The three appeal judges were appalled at the amount of time I had spent in prison and shocked that I had *never* been given an alternative to a prison sentence. I had been lucky to have been granted an appeal at all as people with my sort of record very rarely get the chance to have their appeal heard — it's seen as being a waste of time and money!

The Kathryn Price Hughes Hostel (KPH) had agreed to take me after initially refusing me because of my record and reputation. The appeal judges had replaced my two-year sentence, (of which I had already served ten months) with a three-year probation order and a six months' condition of residence at KPH.

I arrived at KPH exhausted, suspicious and totally paranoid after a very heavy time in prison resulting from being found not guilty at the Snaresbrook trial. I did firmly believe that everyone was out to 'get me'. I put huge bolts on the inside of my door and I used to make up my bed as if a body were in it and, then, sleep under it! I hid in my own wardrobe trembling, waiting, *always* waiting for 'them' to come and 'get me'.

During the day I got drunk; at night I took drugs. I broke all the curfew rules, had screaming temper tantrums, and at times verbally abused everyone in earshot. I wanted them to throw me out. I wanted my safe little cell in the punishment block. My hostel wardens Paul, Lynn, Colin and Liz, took time out for me, made no demands on me and in time trust began to grow. My probation officer Dee did not patronize me. She just let me find myself and get through all the hurting I had suffered and all the walls and defences I had erected over the years. I talked to Dee every week and came to rely more and more on our talks. Gradually the weeks went by and I gained confidence, trust and a sense of humour. I even began to *like* being out of prison!

After I had been out of prison a couple of months I was approached by a woman who seemed to show genuine concern for the situation in women's prisons. I *desperately* wanted to do something. She suggested that she rent a flat for ex-prisoners near to Holloway Prison. The plan was that myself and another ex-prisoner would meet the women coming out of prison each morning and, if they had no place to go to, would invite them to stay at this safe flat, help them with advice on DHSS, accommodation etc. and be generally supportive through the first few months. Just what was needed! I even surprised myself with my enthusiasm! A flat was found and I spent many hours redecorating it and cleaning the carpets. At this time the Greenham women were camping outside Holloway Prison. I gave them a set of keys to the flat and invited them to use it freely. I met Chris Tchaikovsky when she came to visit them at the flat, and she told me about WIP. About this time the woman who had suggested the flat project suddenly lost interest in it. I was given no more money for decorating and I found it more and more difficult to contact the woman who had previously shown such enthusiasm for the project. (Much later I discovered that she is a journalist and that she had been using me to get copy for a couple of articles she eventually had published. I am sorry to have to say that ex-prisoners are often exploited in this way.)

I was offered the chance of a holiday in Ireland with some ex-Greenham women and I was gone! I forgot my conditions of residence and my probation order. The ex-prisoners' flat project had collapsed and I was free to run away to Ireland. Seven weeks later I was in Mountjoy Prison in Dublin, charged with receiving one stolen return ticket home. I had expected Mountjoy to be a tough place but it was OK as far as prisons go. No one threatened, bullied or wound us up. Their whole attitude seemed to be that a contented inmate made for an easier prison to run. There was no cutting-up, no headbanging and no alarm bells. After five days the case was dismissed and I returned home. I went again to WIP and after doing voluntary work with them for a few months was eventually offered a full-time job.

At the time of writing (July 1984) I have been out of prison sixteen months. Looking back over those sixteen months I can begin to see some of the reasons why my life has changed during that time. First, KPH was the ideal setting for me. There I found a structured and supportive setting where, although limits were set, the wardens took time to talk with me and discuss things if I went beyond those limits. They treated me as a rational person who ought to be able to respond to reason; they did not just kick me out, they did not treat me as if I were beyond all help. Getting a job where I could use my intelligence and skills in a useful way was another step in the right direction, though I knew that I had to go slowly, a step at a time. Writing about my prison experiences has also helped me to sort out some things about my past, though it is never easy to use one's private pain to inform a public issue. I still sometimes find it hard to do the things which most people can do without thinking twice, but at least I'm beginning to know how to cope with difficult times. Nowadays, I really think that I have more good times than bad ones. In fact, after all those years inside, and for the first time since I was fourteen, I feel that at last I'm getting control of my life. I'm living now.

Women In Prison

Pat Carlen and Chris Tchaikovsky

In 1970 a Home Office Report predicted that as this century drew to its close fewer women, or maybe no women at all, would be given prison sentences.[1] Twelve years later, in 1982, the daily population of the British women's prisons averaged at around fifteen hundred.[2] The majority of convicted women prisoners are convicted of minor crimes against property; less than ten per cent of convicted and imprisoned women have been found guilty of a crime of violence. A disproportionately high number of women in prison are from ethnic minority groups and in general, as a growing body of research indicates, women are primarily sent to prison because of either their unconventional domestic circumstances, the failure of the non-penal welfare or health institutions to cope with their problems, or their own refusal to comply with socially-conditioned female gender-stereotype requirements.[3] If they are young women whom their parents believe to be beyond control, if they are homeless, if they are single or separated from their husbands, if they have drink or drug-related problems or if their children are in care . . . then they are more likely to go to prison than are women offenders living more conventional lives.[4] Once in prison they will face disciplinary regimes which are much more rigid than those imposed in the men's prisons[5] and this rigidity is a direct result both of the erroneous assumption that most women in prison are maladjusted[6] and of the discriminatory social practices which in general demand higher standards of behaviour of women than of men.[7] Analysis of the regimes in the women's prisons leads us to conclude that the motto of those running them could well be summed up by the slogan 'Discipline, Infantilize, Feminize, Medicalize and Domesticize'.

It is often assumed that women's prisons are sedate places more like young ladies' boarding schools than gaols. This is a myth. It is not only in the men's prisons and the women's borstals that there is a high degree of tension and violence, there is much violence in the adult women's closed prisons. Some of it stems from women who, for a variety of reasons cannot cope with their tension and anxiety in any other way; some of it is officer-provoked through the two ruses of 'winding up' and 'setting-up' (see chapter four); whilst some of the violence is precipitated by young women who, in order to maintain their self-respect, are determined to fight the system. What all women have to face — however they decide to approach their sentence — is a system which engenders in them confused states of consciousness by contradictorily defining them as being both within and without femininity, adulthood and sanity.[8] Women who have never had (and maybe never desired) a house and family are taught domestic skills.[9] Women who do have children are separated from them and yet are at the same time made to feel guilty about that separation.[10] Women who have already rejected conventional and (for them) debilitating female roles are constantly enjoined to 'be feminine' at the same time as they are being denied the sociability with other women prisoners which might in the future enable them to live independently of the male-related domesticity which they have either already rejected or which, on the basis of their experiences, they have come to see as being at least one source of their past difficulties. In addition to using children and family as disciplinary controls on women (see chapter four) the prison also increasingly incorporates into its regime a major method for controlling women outside prison — that is by isolating them from each other. This was true of Scotland's Cornton Vale and it is also true of the 'new' Holloway and Durham's H-Wing.[11] It is a particularly insidious trend in women's imprisonment as it once more denies to the many women who are already leading isolated lives outside prison any legitimate communicative experience other than the weekly trip to the doctor (usually male) for the pharmaceutical fix. Furthermore, women prisoners are made to submit to hundreds of petty rules on the supposition that as women in prison are generally maladjusted and childlike they need strict discipline and constant surveillance.

Now it could, of course, be argued that *all* prisoners, male and female, suffer humiliation through the arbitrary enforcement of innumerable petty rules and we would recognize the justice of that argument. In reply, however, we would argue that male prisoners, being less isolated from each other, are more frequently able to develop a mutually supportive counter-culture which militates against them being so closely supervised as women prisoners. Women prisoners can also be very supportive of each other as we saw in chapters three and four, but because men's prisons are so crowded their officers cannot even begin to attempt to regulate the every movement of the men in the way that officers in the less crowded women's prisons attempt to monitor every move that the women make.[12] Equally, whereas the macho ethic held by some male prisoners means that some of them at least can view prison brutality as a celebration of machismo, women — even those who have rejected the constraining notion of 'femininity' — have no similar, culturally legitimated and romantic self-concept which might enable them to see brutality as an enhancement of their self-image. This is not to say that women prisoners are never violent, it is to argue that they more frequently tend to see brutality for what it is — and fear that they will become brutalized. It is the fear of institutionalization and brutalization, together with the over-rigid discipline, which lead both to the high degree of tension in women's prisons and to the officially recorded fact that the average number of disciplinary charges brought against women prisoners is consistently higher than the number brought against men.[13]

Additionally, (and again, ironically) women prisoners who have been sent to prison because of their already difficult circumstances are both frustrated at being completely powerless to cope with their problems during their term of imprisonment and rendered extremely anxious by the often-worsening domestic circumstances which their imprisonment brings about. Their very imprisonment can trigger-off an onslaught of threats which drive them frantic with worry and fear. There are threats by social workers that they will have the women's children taken into care, threats from husbands that they will divorce them, threats from lovers that they will leave them, threats from housing departments that they will lose their tenancies — and so on. All that the woman prisoner *can* do is to ask for drugs to 'calm her nerves', knowing that when she next walks out through the prison gate all her problems will still be waiting for her and that she, having been made fatter by the drugs and generally debilitated by imprisonment, will be even less able to cope with them. And in connection with drug usage in women's prisons (a question which we discuss more fully on p. 165 in chapter four) the increased risk of institution-generated addictions in teenagers is, of course, yet another reason for responsible people to be appalled at the 77 per cent increase in the numbers of 15 and 16 year old women being given custodial sentences.[14]

There are few legitimate channels via which prisoners can either report abuses or seek effective help for their problems. Consequently, maybe the greatest damage which prison inflicts is that it induces in prisoners a sense of nothingness, a certain knowledge that they will never be believed and never be taken seriously by the prison authorities. As we know from the already well-documented accounts of prison deaths, such powerlessness can have horrifying and even fatal effects in penal institutions where large numbers of physically-ill and mentally and emotionally-disturbed people are routinely being locked up alone in their prison cells.[15]

It was because she was in prison at a time when a woman burned to death in her cell that Chris Tchaikovsky decided that she must begin a campaign to publicize conditions in the women's prisons. That was in 1974 and the immediate result was the formation in Holloway of The Prisoners' Action Group. But it was not until she had finally given up crime (after the death of her father and the birth of a friend's child) and been to University that she was in a position to think once more about a public campaign to right the wrongs of women's imprisonment. The spur to action came in 1982 when she had a chance meeting with another ex-prisoner. Mel told Chris that Holloway was still full of women convicted of minor crimes; women who, for a variety of reasons, should never see the inside of a prison at all. Mel and Chris also discussed Holloway's most recent case of a woman burning to death in her cell. Chris decided that the time had come to act. The Greater London Council's Women's Committee had just been formed, Chris had been elected a member of it and, with the encouragement of its Chair, Valerie Wise, she decided to formulate a grant application which would enable her to launch and staff the Women In Prison campaigning group. Whilst reading the very few books already written on women's prisons she came across Pat Carlen's *Women's Imprisonment* and decided to invite its author to join the Group. However, knowing that only ex-prisoners can fully understand either the brutalizing or debilitating effects that can result from imprisonment, throughout the summer of 1983 Chris worked primarily at establishing or re-establishing contacts with other ex-prisoners. Gradually the nucleus of an active and fully committed Group was established and by October 1983 WIP had formulated a full campaign manifesto (see page 187).

In January 1984 the GLC Women's Committee approved a grant application which allowed WIP to employ a full-time worker and two part-time workers in a job share. Two months later a grant from Islington Council enabled WIP to employ a fourth woman as full-time 'employment development' worker. As three of WIP's four paid workers are women who have served prison sentences they are well placed to engage in the round of lectures on prisons, prison visits, lobbying and general campaigning in which WIP has been involved during its first year of existence. The Group has contacts in all of the women's prisons in England, Wales, Scotland and Northern Ireland and there is always a welcome and practical help available for newly-released women at the WIP offices in Central London. In the past six months these offices have been visited not only by women just out of Holloway Prison but also by women who have been in prisons as far afield as Styal (Cheshire), Cornton Vale (Scotland) and Pucklechurch (Bristol). The Group's steering committee includes women with a diversity of skills — a probation officer, a hostel warden, a teacher, a designer of graphics, an accountant, a lawyer and a journalist. The main bulk of the work, however, is done by the four paid workers. At the time of writing (June 1984) WIP's next planned project is the establishing of an Annexe, a centre where women ex-prisoners can go to meet, talk and engage in leisure pursuits and, if they are so inclined, embark on longer-term skills and education courses.

So, after years of being ignored by the penal reformers, after years of being invisible to the general public, the state of the women's prisons is now, at last, being forced into the arena of penal politics and public debate. We hope that this book will sharpen that debate; we also hope that it will convince the magistracy and the judiciary that it really is time for them to take seriously, and help fulfil, the Home Office's 1970 prediction:

It may be that, as the end of the century draws nearer, penological progress will result in ever fewer or no women at all being given prison sentences.[16]

Appendix

The Women In Prison Manifesto

Why Women In Prison?

During the last decade the number of British women prisoners has increased by 65 per cent. The average daily populations of women in British prisons in 1981 were 1,407 in England and Wales and 135 in Scotland. In 1980 the average daily population of women in prison in Northern Ireland was 69. As prisoners, women suffer the same deprivations, indignities and violations of civil rights as male prisoners. Additionally as *women* in prison they suffer from sexist and racist discriminatory practices which result, for instance, in them receiving fewer leisure, work and educational opportunities, closer surveillance and much greater control by drugs than male prisoners. Yet women prisoners have been largely ignored by prison campaigners, prison writers and officials in the penal and judicial systems. Women In Prison therefore seeks to unite women of all classes, ethnic backgrounds and sexual orientation in a campaign which whilst highlighting, and attempting to redress, the injustices presently suffered by Britain's hitherto neglected women prisoners, will also contribute to the wider campaigns for democratic control of the criminal justice and penal systems.

Women In Prison — campaigning for WOMEN PRISONERS — demands:

1. Improved safety conditions, particularly in Holloway Prison where women have been burned to death in their cells.
2. The introduction of a range of facilities (e.g. more visits, including family and conjugal visits in relaxed surroundings, more association with other prisoners, fewer petty rules)

187

aimed both a reducing tension and, subsequently, the number of drugs prescribed for behaviour and mood control rather than the benefit of prisoners.

3. Improved, non-discriminatory and non-paternalistic education, job-related training, leisure and work facilities.

4. Improved training and supervision of prison officers, aimed at reducing their present discriminatory practices against women from ethnic minorities and lesbian, disabled or mentally or emotionally disturbed women.

5. A mandatory and non-discriminatory income-entitlement to meet the basic needs of women prisoners.

6. Improvement of the existing child-care facilities in prisons together with the introduction of a whole new range of child-care facilities for mothers receiving a custodial sentence (e.g. new centres specially for mothers and children; contacts with local nurseries and parents' groups).

7. Improved medical facilities in general and specialized facilities for women during pregnancy, childbirth and menstruation.

8. Dismantling of the punitive disciplinary structure coupled with the development of official recognition of prisoner participation in the organization of the prison.

9. Non-discriminatory sentencing of women.

10. Unrestricted access to the Boards of Visitors for representatives from women's organizations, community, ethnic minority and other minority (e.g. lesbian) organizations.

Women In Prison — campaigning for ALL PRISONERS — demands:

1. Democratic control of the criminal justice and penal systems with: suspension of Official Secrets Act restrictions on the availability of information about prisons; public accountability of the Home Office Prison Department for its administration of the prisons; public inquiries replacing Home Office internal inquiries into the deaths of prisoners, injuries and complaints in general together with Legal Aid to enable prisoners' families to be represented at any such inquiry.

2. Reduction in the length of prison sentences.

3. Replacement of the parole system with the introduction of half-remission on all sentences. Access to a sentence-review panel after serving seven years of a life sentence.

4. Increased funding for non-custodial alternatives to prisons (e.g. community service facilities, sheltered housing, alcohol recovery units) together with greater use of the existing sentencing alternatives (e.g. deferred sentence, community service order, probation with a condition of psychiatric treatment etc.), with the aim of removing from prisons all who are there primarily because of drunkenness, drug dependency, mental, emotional or sexual problems, homelessness or inability to pay a fine.

5. Abolition of the censorship of prisoners' mail.

6. Abolition of the Prison Medical Service and its replacement by normal National Health Service provision coupled with abolition of the present system whereby prison officers vet, and have the power to refuse, prisoners' requests to see a doctor.

7. Provision of a law library in prisons so that prisoners may have access to information about their legal rights in relation to DHSS entitlement, employment, housing, marriage and divorce, child-custody, court proceedings, debt, prison rules etc.

8. Improved living and sanitary conditions together with a mandatory income entitlement to meet basic needs.

9. Non-discretionary rights to call witnesses and to full legal representation of prisoners at Visiting (internal) Court proceedings together with the abolition of the charge of 'making false and malicious allegations against an officer.'

10. A review of the existing methods of the recruitment and training of prison discipline staff.

Information about The Women In Prison Campaign can be obtained from:

WIP, Unit 3, Cockpit Yard,
Northington Street, London WC1N 2NP
Tel: 01-430 0767/8

Notes

Introduction

1. Good reviews of these theories are to be found in: C. Smart (1976) *Women, Crime and Criminology: A Feminist Critique*, London, Routledge and Kegan Paul; L. Crites (1976) *The Female Offender*, Massachusetts, Lexington Books; F. Adler and R. Simon (1979) *The Criminology of Deviant Women*, Boston, Houghton Mifflin.
2. C. Lombroso and W. Ferrero (1895) *The Female Offender*, London, Fisher Unwin.
3. W. I. Thomas (1907) *Sex and Society*, Boston, Little Brown.
4. W. I. Thomas (1923) *The Unadjusted Girl*, New York, Harper and Row.
5. P. Carlen (1983) *Women's Imprisonment*, London, Routledge and Kegan Paul.
6. See D. P. Farrington and A. Morris (1983a) 'Sex, Sentencing and Reconviction', *British Journal of Criminology*, 23/3 (July): 229−248; D. P. Farrington and A. Morris (1983b) 'Do Magistrates Discriminate against Men?', *Justice of the Peace*, 17 September: 601−603; and A. Worrall (1981) 'Out of Place: The Female Offender in Court', *Probation Journal* 28: 90−93.
7. O. Pollak (1950) *The Criminality of Women*, Philadelphia, University of Pennsylvania Press.
8. See P. Carlen (1983) op. cit.
9. S. Box (1983) *Power, Crime and Mystification*, London, Tavistock, p. 166.
10. S. Box (1983) op. cit.: 168.
11. S. Box (1983) op. cit.: 173.
12. For examples see M. Chesney-Lind (1974) 'Juvenile Delinquency: The Sexualisation of Female Crime', *Psychology Today*, 7: 43−6; A. Conway and C. Bogdan (1977) 'Sexual Delinquency: The Persistence of a Double-Standard', *Crime and Delinquency* 23: 131−42; and

L. Shacklady-Smith (1978) 'Sexist Assumptions and Female Delinquency' in C. and B. Smart (eds) (1978) *Women, Sexuality and Social Control*, London, Routledge and Kegan Paul.

13. S. Box (1983) op. cit.: 170.
14. J. Cowie, V. Cowie and E. Slater (1968) *Delinquency in Girls*, London, Heinemann.
15. F. Heidensohn (1968) 'The Deviance of Women: A Critique and an Enquiry', *British Journal of Sociology*, 19/2.
16. C. and B. Smart (eds) (1978) op. cit.
17. F. Adler (1975) *Sisters in Crime*, New York, McGraw Hill; R. Simon (1975) *Women and Crime*, Massachusetts, Lexington Books.
18. C. Smart (1976) op. cit.: 74.
19. For an excellent discussion of the possible effects of racism on lawbreaking and criminalization see, J. Lea and J. Young (1984) *What is to be Done about Law and Order?* Harmondsworth, Penguin.
20. M. Cousins (1980) 'Mens Rea: A Note on Sexual Difference, Criminology and the Law', in P. Carlen and M. Collison (1980) *Radical Issues in Criminology*, Oxford, Martin Robertson.
21. M. Cousins (1980) op. cit.: 117.
22. We also know from unofficial sources that there are disproportionate numbers of women from ethnic minority groups in prison.
23. See Carlen (1983) op. cit.; Farrington and Morris (1983a, 1983b) op. cit.; and Worrall (1981) op. cit.
24. T. C. N. Gibbens (1971) 'Female Offenders', *British Journal of Hospital Medicine*, September.
25. NACRO (1984) *Monitoring The Criminal Justice Act*, April, London, National Association for the Care and Rehabilitation of Offenders.

Chapter 1

1. This is my real name, it is not a pseudonym.
2. A10 was a branch of the Metropolitan Police set up in 1972 by Sir Robert Mark to investigate all complaints against Metropolitan Officers. For a fuller account see B. Cox, J. Shirley, M. Short (1977) *The Fall of Scotland Yard*, Harmondsworth, Penguin.

Chapter 2

1. Diana is the name which her parents gave her; Christina is the name which she gave herself.
2. Children who lived in council flats owned by the London County Council.
3. Whenever the term Smoking is used with a capital S in this article it refers to the smoking of marihuana.

Chapter 3

1. Direct Mail firms are firms which specialize in compiling mailing lists and whose business consists of advertising clients' products and services by post.

Chapter 4

1. L. Taylor, R. Lacey and D. Bracken (1979) *In Whose Best Interest?* London, Cobden Trust/MIND.
2. J. Boyle (1977) *A Sense of Freedom,* Edinburgh, Canongate.
3. The Criminal Justice Act 1982 replaced Borstal training with the youth custody sentence. Under the Act all Borstals became Youth Custody Centres.
4. Evidence that people are frightened for their lives in British prisons is given in G. Coggan and M. Walker (1982) *Frightened For My Life,* London, Fontana, a book which, regrettably, does not deal with deaths in women's prisons. For an account of deaths in women's prisons see M. Benn and C. Ryder-Tchaikovsky (1983) 'Women Behind Bars', in *New Statesman,* 9 December.
5. Report on the Work of The Prison Department 1982 (1983) *CMND 9057* HMSO London.
6. There is some evidence that the trend in women's imprisonment is towards women being held both under greater surveillance and in greater isolation from each other. Pat Carlen found this to be the case in the Scottish Women's prison at Cornton Vale, Stirling (see P. Carlen (1983) op. cit.) whilst Josie O'Dwyer suggests that the living arrangements at the 'new' Holloway are indicative of the same trend. She writes:

> The old Holloway had a different feel about it. I'm not saying that it was a sort of haven because it wasn't. It was old, smelly, rat-infested and people would actually shit in newspapers and throw them out of the windows because they couldn't stand the smell in the cells all night. But you could see what was going on. If another inmate was upset you could see it and say, 'Come on, come and have a roll-up with me.' You could help each other. There were only two officers to supervise seventy-five inmates. Nowadays there's four of them to every twenty-five of you. There's toilets in your cell, a sink and slatted windows, but it's harder. You're all on top of one another like in a battery hen enclosure. So it's claustrophobic and yet at the same time you're

all separated from each other. It's all narrow corridors and everything and everyone is round a corner. You can hear the screaming and the shouting but you can no longer see what is going on.

Chapter 5

1. Home Office (1970) *Treatment of Women and Girls in Custody*, London, Prison Department.
2. Home Office (1983) *Report on the Work of the Prison Department CMND 9057*, London, HMSO; Northern Ireland Office (1982) *Report on the Administration of the Prison Service*, London, HMSO; Scottish Home And Health Department (1983) *Report on Prisons in Scotland, 1982.*
3. See P. Carlen (1983) op. cit.
4. See D. P. Farrington and A. Morris (1983a and b) op. cit.; A. Worrall (1981) op. cit.
5. M. Fitzgerald and J. Sim (1979) *British Prisons*, Oxford, Basil Blackwell.
6. See C. Smart (1976) op. cit.
7. See B. Hutter and G. Williams (eds) (1981) *Controlling Women*, London, Croom Helm.
8. See P. Carlen (1983) op. cit.
9. See M. Benn (1984) 'Marking Time', *New Statesman*, 15th June; A. Smith (1962) *Women in Prison*, London, Stevens; P. Carlen (1983) op. cit.
10. See P. Carlen (1983) op. cit.
11. See J. Ward (1984) 'Exploding the Myth', *The Abolitionist*, July.
12. See chapter three of this book and P. Carlen (1983) op. cit.
13. See M. Fitzgerald and J. Sim (1979) op. cit.; R. Smith (1984) 'Women in Prison.' *British Medical Journal*, February 25th; Home Office (1983) op. cit.
14. See NACRO (1984) op. cit.
15. See M. Benn and C. Ryder-Tchaikovsky (1983) op. cit.
16. Home Office (1970) op. cit.

Index

THE
NORTHERN COLLEGE
LIBRARY
50699
BARNSLEY